A HOUSE INTERRUPTED

A Wife's Story of Recovering from Her Husband's Sex Addiction

MAURITA CORCORAN

A HOUSE INTERRUPTED

A Wife's Story of Recovering from Her Husband's Sex Addiction

MAURITA CORCORAN

Gentle Path
P R E S S

Carefree, Arizona

Gentle Path Press
P.O. Box 3172
Carefree, Arizona 85377
www.gentlepath.com

First Edition: 2011

For more information regarding our publications, please contact
Gentle Path Press at 1-800-708-1796 (toll-free U.S. only).

Book edited by Rebecca Post
Book designed by Serena Castillo

ISBN: 978-0-9826505-8-5

Author's Note: Most names have been changed in this book to protect the
confidentiality of the author's family members, friends, and acquaintances
in recovery. In some cases, real names have been used with the permission of
those individuals. Certain circumstances and names of places have also been
changed to preserve the privacy of people who appear in this book.

To my four children, the bright lights and great loves of my life.
Miracles do happen and people can change.

And to my husband, you were right:
Marrying you has been a wild ride.
Thank you for your complete, unwavering support
and patience throughout the writing of this project.

I love you more now than ever before.

Contents

Introduction

In August of 1997, my husband of fourteen years disclosed to me his addiction to sex. I had never heard of such an addiction and was completely blindsided by the double life he had been living—right behind my reasonably educated back. Hearing the truth about my marriage—rampant infidelity and other dark, sexual behaviors—was devastating, traumatic, and catapulted me into a journey of recovery. This was a journey of excruciating pain and difficult self-examination, but it eventually resulted in my rebirth as a new woman.

This book is based on the detailed journals I kept during the beginning years of my recovery. I tried to choose entries that paint an accurate picture of what it was like to learn the unthinkable and to walk through the deserts of grief, anger, resentment, self-pity, and victimization. I decided to keep the bulk of my journal entries raw and uncensored in form. If you are a wife or partner who is just learning about sex addiction, I want you to take comfort in realizing you are not alone on this path. Your feelings of shock, anger, and grief are normal.

Now for the good news. I want you to know that there will be eventual healing and a light at the end of the tunnel if you are willing to take the steps to heal yourself from betrayal. For me, my emotional recovery began after I got over the shock and trauma at what had happened to my marriage and I began looking at myself, my own choices and behaviors. I instinctively knew I had to ask myself the big question: What is up with me that I would marry a sex addict?

In the following pages you will learn about what happened to my life when I found out about my husband's sexual addiction and my road back to a new-found spiritual and emotional recovery. My life today is proof that you do not have to stay broken when infidelity and sex addiction strike out at your heart. It is possible to reclaim your spirit and heal your soul.

Brace yourself. If you are the spouse or partner of a sex addict, the journey in facing the truth about your life can be arduous and painful. I can promise you that, at times, the healing process will be lonely. There will be times in your healing when only you alone can do the necessary work to move forward. No therapist, no minister, no friend, and no husband can walk with you.

Most of all, know and remember this: You are worth every bit of the effort that this process asks of you. You are worth the time it takes to recover your sanity, your balance on Earth, and your spirit so that you can be whole again.

ಞಿ

Part One: Hell on Earth

ಞಿ

Chapter One. The Set Up

ℰℴℭℛ

My life took a dramatic, unimaginable turn after a phone call from my husband, fourteen years into our marriage. Before I get to that night, allow me to share with you my personal background and some early life experiences.

I was born and raised in Wellesley, Massachusetts, an affluent suburb west of Boston, home of Wellesley College for women. The first house I can remember was quite small. But the second house, on Abbott Road, was enormous with three stories, nineteen rooms, five bathrooms, six fireplaces, and a barn. The Wellesley Country Club was at the end of Abbott Road and across the street from Babson College. I spent a great deal of time at the country club while I was growing up, and my father spent every weekend for twenty years on that golf course. We were a large family, and I was the middle child with three sisters—two older, one younger—and a younger brother.

My first significant memories are of my father. I remember sitting on a bicycle at the top of our inclined driveway at our first house on Weston Road. I must have been four or five years old and so short that my feet didn't quite reach the pedals. My father put me on the bike seat, gave me a little shove, and I pedaled. I ran smack into the garage door, fell over, got up, walked the bike back up the slight incline of our driveway, and my dad put me back on the seat so I could do the same thing over again. I learned to ride a bike in two days. My Dad was firm but gentle with me, encouraging me to try again after I steered the bicycle into the bushes, into the garage, or toppled it on the grass. I remember wanting so badly to be able to ride that bike, for me and for him. From a very early age, I always felt this intense need to get his attention, his approval, his love.

When my parents first bought the house on the hill on Abbott Road, my father called it the "the worst house in the nicest neighborhood." The previous owners had let it go, and the vines that covered the row of second-story windows gave the house a look of being swallowed. It was so overgrown that that you could barely see the first two floors from the street.

In that neighborhood, we grew up surrounded by affluence in a truly beautiful area. Most of the families had many kids; the family across the street had ten children. My best friends—Nancy Arnot, Pam Pierson and Debbie Babson—all lived within four or five houses of each other on Abbott Road. At least six families on Abbott Road had a doctor as the head of the household.

My early feelings or thoughts of my mother are not as clear. My first real memory of her was some time after we moved to the Abbott road house. After dinner in the evenings, we would get together with the neighborhood kids to play baseball in one of two small neighborhood parks. One night they needed a pitcher and an older boy put me on the mound. When I pitched the first ball, a boy hit a ground ball, it bounced off my toe and into my face, breaking my nose. A big deal was made over it and I remember a day later, sitting in the surgeon's waiting room, listening to my mother tell another person about my accident. She was animated and I remember a feeling of deep concern for my well-being—not necessarily love, but serious, honest concern. After my nose was reset, my sisters each took me into their classrooms for show and tell. I stood there with two black eyes and a bandage over my nose as the first and second graders stared up at me and listened to my sisters' version of my accident.

My parents were hardworking. My father was dedicated to his growing insurance business, community service, and his lifelong passion for golf. What time he did seem to spend with us was usually focused on my brother, David, his only son. My mother was equally dedicated to keeping a beautiful home, raising well-rounded children, and pursuing her creative and artistic talents. She enjoyed creative pursuits, taking art classes or cooking classes, and she was always willing to try just about anything new to her.

We were Sunday churchgoers from day one until I went to high school. Because of those early years of Sunday Mass and Sunday School, I have always felt at home in the Catholic Church; however,

I never did develop a deep spiritual connection to the Catholic faith. As soon as my parents stopped making Sunday Mass mandatory, I stopped going to church. By the time I left for college, my spiritual foundation was nonexistent.

I have come to learn that my family was quite different from how we must have appeared to onlookers. Inside that big house on the hill, we were strangers to one another, not able to connect with each other on an intimate, openly loving level. My siblings and I certainly had a lot of fun together growing up. Our house was always humming with activity, and I especially remember our high school years full of girlfriends and boyfriends, coming and going. On the outside we were happy and involved with a lot of after school functions, like cheerleading and other sports. But for the most part, we lived on the surface of our emotions, especially toward our parents.

My father's business turned out to be a great success, so my parents were able to provide for all my financial needs. They were not, however, available to me on a deep emotional or spiritual level. I felt they never expected anything out of me except to go to college and get married. So that is exactly what I did.

By the time I was a freshman in college, I had started a pattern of allowing whomever I was dating to shape the path of my life. I didn't realize it then, but I needed a man in my life to define me—I was not worthy enough in my own right. Because I felt pushed aside and was emotionally neglected by my father, I gravitated to men who were both driven and focused (as my father was), but these men were also distant and emotionally uninvolved with me. It was the perfect set up to marry an addict.

I started college with no clear vision for what I wanted to do with my life. I was interested in politics, retail, and journalism, but I had no idea what definite path to choose. I just went about life at that age with little planning, lots of spontaneity, and no thought about what kind of woman I wanted to be. Some people would consider that a free spirit. In retrospect, however, I wasn't free at all. I had no clue that the very essence of who I was born to be was already slipping away, even at that young age. Unaware of what I wanted or where I was going, I simply moved on.

After finishing my second year at Centenary College for Women in New Jersey, I left the East Coast for the mountain town of Boulder, Colorado, outside of Denver. I wanted to ski, so I transferred to the University of Colorado, even though I didn't know a soul there.

Boulder in the mid-1970s, had such a bohemian and appealing atmosphere. The temperature warms in midday, never getting too hot or humid. Once the morning clouds clear off the flatirons, the pure blue sky is stunning. I lounged in that mountain setting, studying class schedules and writing letters to girlfriends. It was late August and students at the university milled around The Hill, a quaint business district just off campus. It seemed like everyone was moving a sofa into a new apartment, out of an old house, or onto a roof. On the outdoor terrace by the pool on campus, it was crowded with students sitting in the sunshine and fresh air. I sat alone, excited to be so far from home and enjoying my independence.

I had been at the school for just two days when I met Ben on the deck of the pool. I had found two chairs to set up camp, one for me and one to prop my feet. From across the way I noticed a handsome, dark-haired guy holding a clip board and walking toward me. He was smiling slightly, wearing dark Ray Bans and red lifeguard shorts. He looked like he'd just stepped off the beach, leaving behind the salt water for this student-filled pool in the mountains of Colorado. While he seemed nice enough and was good looking, I wasn't looking to get involved. It was the furthest thing from my mind.

"Is anyone sitting here?" he asked, putting his hand on the back of the chair that held my feet.

"Yes, there is," I lied.

"No, there isn't," he said.

"Yes. Yes, there is," I shot back.

"I've been watching you," he said. "And as long as I've been watching, no one has sat here with you." He pulled the chair out from under my feet and sat down right across from me. He was so confident with those Ray Bans covering his eyes.

" What's your name?" he asked.

"Wheatsy," I answered, without explanation. He looked at me with a frown.

"What kind of name is that! Wheatsy?"

I put down the letter I was writing so I could answer him.

"When I was little, my sisters couldn't pronounce my real name, Maurita, so they called me Wheata, which stuck and eventually became Wheatsy."

"Wheatsy," he repeated.

"Yes, Wheatsy," I replied, somewhat annoyed. Why am I defending my name to this stranger?, I thought to myself.

"I've just never heard that name before, not even as a nickname."

"Well, what is your name?" I asked.

"Ben."

"Ben?" I responded. "What kind of name is that? Ben? I have never heard of that name before."

"What are you talking about? Ben is a common name," he said, thinking I was serious. I told him I was just kidding, and we smiled at each other. We continued talking and spent most of the afternoon discussing the East Coast and our majors.

"Why are you carrying a clipboard?" I asked.

"I am filling out medical school applications." He gave me a quick glance and continued filling out paperwork, and I went back to writing my letters. We sat through the early sunny evening like that, a nineteen-year old girl in a new college town and a New Jersey lifeguard on the prowl.

"Would you like to have dinner with me this weekend?" he asked as he stood up.

I didn't hesitate.

"Yes, I would," I said. What's a girl to lose having dinner with an attractive man possibly headed for medical school? Nothing. It seemed so at the time. Eventually, though, I nearly lost everything.

Two days later we went on our first date. Classes had not yet started, so each of our schedules was open. We had made plans for dinner. I remember feeling excited and a little nervous. He picked me up at my dorm room and we got into the bucket seats of his light blue Oldsmobile Starfire and drove into downtown Boulder for dinner at the Walrus Restaurant. It was a popular spot but not typical college fare. We had a nice time and we talked a lot about his family, my family, growing up, and how we came to be in Boulder. He was a senior, and I was a third year transfer student.

After dinner, he drove me up to scenic Flagstaff Mountain, just west of downtown Boulder where the flat plains meet the first foothills of the Rockies. Ben parked on the side of the road, and we got out for a while, taking in the spectacular view of downtown. I remember thinking it was so beautiful looking down on Boulder and the lights below and how lucky I was to be there. Then we stopped at Chautauqua Park on the way down from the mountain. Toward the end of the evening, Ben tried several times to do more than just kiss me—I had to keep brushing him off and telling him no. He eventually dropped me off at my dorm room and we kissed good night.

From that night forward, we were pretty much inseparable. We certainly liked each other, but I do not think that either of us at the time thought, *This is the one.* I liked him and thought we had a lot in common: we were both from the East Coast, we both loved to ski and swim, and we both liked the outdoors.

For the next eight years, we pursued one another around the country with me doing most of the chasing. We dated that first year while we were in college. Then, when Ben graduated from CU, I moved back East, where he went to medical school and I went to work in the hotel industry after a brief stint at the Fashion Institute of Technology in New York City. Ben attended St. George's University School of Medicine in the British West Indies. We dated on and off during those years, both of us living elsewhere and experiencing what the world had to offer us. He was deeply invested in medical school, the ensuing internship, and then his residency. Putting my life on hold for those years while he had little or no time for a relationship, didn't make sense to me. So we started seeing other people.

It was while I worked as a concierge in the lobby at the historic Parker House in downtown Boston that I met Keith Knudsen, one of the original Doobie Brothers. I recognized some of his fellow band members from my album covers, but I did not know who Keith was. He introduced himself to me at my desk and we chatted for a few minutes. Quite unexpectedly, he invited me to their concert at the Cape. He seemed very sweet and down to earth, so I said "yes." I gave him directions to my apartment and as he walked away, I asked him what he did. With a smile, he quietly said, "I'm a drummer and I do some vocals."

"Oh," was all I could manage to say.

I was living in Brookline, a town outside of Boston at the time. I lived in a three bedroom apartment on the third floor of a house in a working class section of town. It was a great place, very nice and clean. I lived with one of my college roommates from Centenary and another girl who was a graduate student at Boston University. Keith picked me up that night in a limo and we drove all the way to the Cape—just the two of us. The band was touring for their "Minute by Minute" album. I was so nervous and excited that night.

On the way to the concert we made small talk, then I picked up one of the Minute by Minute albums that he had on the seat next to him and asked, "So, which one of you guys are related? Which ones are the brothers?"

He smiled and said, "None of us are related. There are no real brothers in the group."

"Oh, wow, I didn't know that," I said. Then I took out the album insert and pointed to it and said, "I have never really understood why you would put a picture of a piece of burning trash on this sleeve. What is the significance of that?"

Keith looked at me for a second, threw his head back, and laughed—not in a mean way, but in a gentle, funny way. "Maurita, that's not a trash bag, that's a doobie, a joint. That's where the name the Doobie Brothers comes from."

"Oh," I laughed right along with him because I had no idea.

We had a great time that night and the evening ended very late with a goodnight kiss at my apartment door. That began an almost two year on-again, off-again relationship. I had grown up with money, but nothing like this lifestyle of private planes, limousines, and luxury hotels. We were both honest that first night; he explained he was separated from his wife and in the beginning process of divorce, but he was also seeing other people. I told him about Ben and him being in medical school, so we both just took the relationship as it came. I had no illusions about where my relationship with Keith would end up, so I just went along with it. I saw him pretty much anytime he was near the East Coast. He would leave me a ticket at the counter at Logan Airport, and I would fly off to be with him on tour—sometimes for a weekend, sometimes for as long as five days. I went with him to Philadelphia, New York, Connecticut, Cape Cod, Montreal, and Nova Scotia. I even flew a couple of times on the Doobie Liner, as they called their private plane with their familiar logo was on its tail.

I enjoyed the attention and excitement for a while, and when Keith said he had fallen in love with the woman with whom I believe eventually became his second wife, I was sad, of course, but happy to have had such a great time while it lasted. My pattern of finding comfort in the shadows of unavailable men continued with Keith, and what a shadow that was.

Moreover, there is something about me that addicts are attracted to and something about me that makes me attracted to addicts. My father was distant, and addicts are typically distant. This emotional disconnect is what I was familiar and comfortable with. It is no accident that I would someday marry someone who steered away from intimacy. And it is no accident that I got involved with Keith, who would someday battle his own addictive demons.

I didn't see Keith Knudsen again until the summer before Ben's disclosure to me about his sex addiction. The Doobie Brothers were touring again and playing in Myrtle Beach. I took Ben, our oldest daughter, Ella, and my nephew to the concert. Keith invited us backstage after the concert. It was great to see him again. He looked happy and healthy and gave the kids signed t-shirts and drumsticks. Ben took the kids back out on the field, and I sat down with Keith for a few minutes. He was happily remarried, and he had been in recovery for eight years. That was news to me; when I dated him I did not realize that he was an addict. We got up and gave each other a hug and that was it. I never saw him again.

Then, in February of 2005, Ben was watching CNN and learned that Keith had died of complications due to chronic pneumonia. It was a difficult loss for me as I had always hoped to talk face to face with him again—but this time as two people in recovery.

Eventually, Ben and I got back together, better than before. That was during his three year-long residency in Baltimore. The weather had already gotten cold that year as I was preparing to go north to Wellesley for the Thanksgiving holiday.

"I have something for you," Ben told me. It was almost midnight. I had just gotten home from working the evening shift at the Hyatt Regency Baltimore where I was an assistant front office manager, and I still had to pack for an early morning flight.

I sat down next to Ben and looked at him and said, "What is it?"

In his hand, he held a small, velvet ring box. He handed it to me to open. I opened it and it was an engagement ring.

I asked, "Is this an engagement ring? Are we getting married?"

He said, "Yeah, I want to marry you, but I haven't really thought about when."

I was a bit shocked. I was happy that he gave me a ring, but I was a little confused about the lack of a proposal or planning. I put the ring on my finger and thought, Ok—*now I am engaged.*

I didn't realize then, only later, that he never actually asked me to marry him. He offered me jewelry, which I accepted, but he never said the words, *Will you marry me?* We did not discuss wedding plans for a year or so. For his third year of residency, Ben chose a hospital in Rochester, New York. As a woman engaged to a doctor, I finally felt comfortable telling my parents that this time when we moved, we would be living together. My father vowed to cease speaking to me on religious grounds, and while my mother continued to take my phone calls, they were short, one-sided conversations.

"He'll never marry you," she'd say. Or, "He's using you," and "You're living in sin and he's Jewish. When he gets what he wants from you, he will dump you for a Jewish girl."

This was a stressful and painful period for me. For the first time in my life, my father was not just a phone call away, the one consistent, constant in my life—distant perhaps, but certainly constant. He literally would not speak to me as long as I was living with Ben. My mother almost always ended our conversations by beating me down, telling me I was a fool. She never believed he would marry me.

After two years with no wedding plans on the horizon, I played the only card I had left to play. Over dinner in downtown Rochester, I laid out an ultimatum.

"Either we set a date or I'm out of here," I told him.

"Then, we'll set a date," he said casually, between bites of his steak. "How is May or June?"

"Too far away. How's November?" I asked. "We can have the ceremony the day before Thanksgiving and then everyone can just stay for dinner the following day."

"Fine, sounds good," he said.

Even with minimal wedding plans, there was still disappointment. That was the year Boston got socked in two days before Thanksgiving with a huge snow storm, stranding some of my family and friends. That left only Ben's creepy friends from Ocean City, his and my immediate families, and one of his doctor friends who served as his best man. At this point, I had this feeling of just wanting to get this wedding over with.

After a quick ceremony in the lobby of the Strathallan Hotel in Rochester, New York, by a justice of the peace who wore cowboy boots under his robe, we were officially and legally married. A month later, I was pregnant with Ella, and a month after that we had a quasi-honeymoon where we went skiing for a week in Aspen, Colorado. Ben, for some reason, invited his father along. *Absurd* is the only word I can think of to describe that trip. I had morning sickness all day long and the hotel room had just one bed. Ben's father slept on a pullout sofa bed in the same room. I had no privacy.

We packed what belongings we'd amassed together in Rochester and moved to the coast of South Carolina to start our family. This was July of 1984. My parents were pleased that the globetrotting had stopped and we were settling down and having children.

Ben joined a busy medical practice on the south end of the beach and I jumped in to setting up our first house and caring for our baby daughter. We had four children over the next six years which became my full time occupation, and happily so. Ben eventually opened his own practice and brought in his first associate. His practice took off like wildfire, taking away our financial worries and allowing us a few luxuries. We would eventually hire a live-in nanny, a weekly housekeeper, and a landscaper, and we owned three cars.

I ran the books, and over the period of several successful years it became clear that we could afford something I have always dreamed of: a house on the beach. Although Ben is well known in town as being a successful physician, on the beach it is another story. There he is best known for his long swims—a mile a day—when the water is warm enough.

"You going to start swimming soon, Doc?" the locals regularly ask him in the latter months of spring. Even the bank tellers at the drive-thru window ask, "Hey Maurita, is your husband in the water yet?" He swam directly in front of our house, near the Surfside Pier, to a restaurant on the beach called the Conch Café, and then ran back on the sand. To some in town, when they see Ben swimming, it is a sign that summer has officially started. His patients seem to like the fact that their doctor practices what he preaches—exercising and taking good care of his body.

After a couple of months of looking at properties up and down the coast, our realtor showed us a faded white box on stilts, just a thousand square feet, nestled into the beach background. It was already furnished with an eclectic array of castoff furniture, comfortable and welcoming.

I loved this little beach house and moved the family over for weekends and off season months any chance we could get. We rented it out for the summer months as we needed the rental income. I always felt a sigh of relief and peace as I drove up into that little driveway. Even though our main home was just five minutes away, the minute I walked up the grey, weather-beaten staircase, I felt that we were away on vacation. The beach house, the little slice of sand dunes, and the magnificent, unobstructed view of the ocean was a tremendous gift, one that I never took for granted. I felt as though I had become a part of this house, and it had become a part of me. Together, we faced the ocean from the same vantage point, and we victoriously weathered the storms.

Unfortunately, our financial success had come at a price. Ben's work and on-call schedule left him no real time for his growing family and me. At times, I felt like a single mother. I had been given the gift of financial security, but I had no one to share it with. We were both so busy living our lives we never invested any time to maintain and develop our emotional connections or respond to each other on an intimate level. I thought our sex life was good, considering the demands on the both of us. When I was even eight and a half months pregnant, he was all over me. Some women complained that their husbands won't touch them during pregnancy. Not mine. That's one of the reasons I never suspected his involvement with other women.

Still, during the times we did spend together, I sometimes felt that something was not quite right. I felt in my gut that he was running from something. Ben was the type of person for whom professional success wasn't enough. He had to always push himself further than his friends were willing to push. He had to run further, row harder, bungee jump higher (or backwards!)—anything to prove himself or be the center of attention.

The summer of 1997 was when everything crashed in one cataclysmic moment, changing the reality I knew. The integral pieces of our lives shattered, and we spent the next ten years trying to mend our hearts and our marriage.

It began to unravel during a family trip to La Jolla, California, where Ben's cousin, Jeff, was getting married on the beach. Ben was an usher, and our youngest daughter, Olivia, was flower girl. What should have been a nice family vacation instead started the downward spiral of our marriage.

The wedding was straight out of a fairy tale. Jeff and his bride were married on the beautiful cliff at Pillbox Park overlooking the Pacific Ocean just north of La Jolla. They pledged their lives to one another and everyone clapped and celebrated with them. It was a beautiful, joyful scene.

Ben looked handsome in his tuxedo, but he always looks handsome when he's dressed up. As the wife of a physician, I'd been to my share of black-tie fundraisers and cocktail parties. I have spent some of those evenings in a gown, on the arm of my attractive husband in his striking tuxedo.

But I was not on his arm at the ceremony, because I was not in the wedding party. Instead, Ben escorted a buxom, long-legged brunette. He seemed to be very pleased to be partnered with a pretty, young woman. She was, in fact, married and had three young children and a nice, good-looking husband. I didn't give her much thought as she had a beautiful family of her own. Plus, she wore way too much make-up—something my husband had always declared a turn off.

The evening of the wedding, before the reception started, we went back to Jeff's house to change clothes and relax for a few moments before the party started. Ben had been drinking and smoking pot all afternoon. I remember standing with some people in the yard taking photographs when Ben popped his head out of the upstairs bedroom window with a lost look on his face.

"Honey," he hollered out toward the gathering below, "come help me."

I looked up and raised my voice so he could hear. "What is it?" I asked.

"I need help. Can you come up here?"

I headed upstairs. When I walked into the bedroom, he was trying to change his trousers. In his inebriated state, he could not get his legs into his pants.

"You've got to save me," he said. "That bridesmaid—she's out to get me. She's giving me the eye," and then he pointed to one of his eyes.

"You're wasted right now." I told him. "Do you realize that? It's embarrassing."

"Ah, c'mon, honey. I'm just having some fun. Don't be such a drag."

I left him there in the upstairs bedroom and returned to the party, determined not to let his ridiculous behavior ruin a wonderful evening.

The next afternoon we all gathered at Jeff and Cathy's house again, this time for a brunch-style meal where the bride and groom would open their wedding gifts. Our four kids were running about the house, playing with the other kids. Every once in a while they'd tear through the living room where the adults had gathered for the gift reception. Lo and behold, there sat my husband next to the woman who had been the bridesmaid the night before. It was noon, and they were already drinking and giggling with each other.

"Ben," I said two or three times, trying to get his attention. "Can I talk to you for a second out on the porch?"

"Sure," he said.

Once outside, I asked him in a hushed whisper, "What the hell are you doing? You're drunk and stoned already and you're making a fool out of yourself with that bridesmaid from yesterday. What do you think you are doing, acting like that?"

"You're overreacting and paranoid," he said. "Nothing is going on."

He turned and walked back into the room as if it was his day and his party. He slid right back down in his seat next to the bridesmaid. I watched them through a window from the porch as they giggled and whispered into each other's ears. I was too humiliated and angry to return to the party.

When the two of them stood up and started heading for the stairs, my heart started pounding. There they were, wading through friends and family—including their own children—and heading upstairs for God knows what. I followed them and halfway up the staircase, I stopped them.

I did not want to cause a scene so my voice was very low, but very deliberate. I said it directly to my husband—I could have cared less what that bridesmaid had to say.

"Where do you think you are going?" I hissed.

"We're just going into the bathroom to get high," Ben answered.

"Oh, no you're not," I said. "We are leaving. Now. Let's go."

He gave the bridesmaid a little shrug, we collected the kids and we left the party. I was devastated. Alarm bells were going off in my head, and I knew then that something was horribly wrong between us. I wrote off some of Ben's behavior to the alcohol, pot, and his need to blow off steam after months of long hours at the hospital and office. But there was plenty of serious doubt left over. I was still upset the next morning when we went for a long run on the beach at Torrey Pines. I could not stop crying. My journal entry surrounding this day follows.

July 10, 1997

...Ben acted so embarrassing and humiliating with a
cosmetically altered mother of three—in front of his
own parents and sister and me, not to mention his
own four children. For the first time in my life I was
truly disgusted with him and wanted nothing to do
with him. The pain he causes me now is greater than
the joy he brings me.

On our flight home from California we were sitting together in
first class and our kids were safely out of earshot in coach. Something
had snapped deep in my soul. I told Ben that he had two weeks to find
himself a serious therapist and get help or he had to move out of the
house. I do not know where I came up with the two weeks. It seemed
a reasonable amount of time for him to find someone and commit to
working on himself. I also think I was trying to buy myself some time
too—to be comfortable with the ultimatum I had just issued.

The ultimatum appeared to sink in, because Ben immediately
started seeing a therapist, Harold Brown, Jr. His credentials were
impressive; he is a Licensed Professional Counselor, a Masters
Addictions Counselor, and a Certified Sexual Addiction Therapist.
After Ben's session with Harold, describing the events of his behavior
at the wedding, this therapist scheduled a joint session to discuss
general issues surrounding our marriage, the wedding, and a course of
action for the coming months.

I readily agreed to go although I was feeling very nervous
being in a therapist's office. I sat down next to Ben on the therapist's
green leather couch. Harold got right to the point and started asking
me a series of questions. "Maurita, I want you to answer the following
questions for me with a simple 'yes' or 'no' answer. I just ask that you
answer as honestly as you can."

"OK," I said. But I remember thinking that my husband's
therapist looked so young. *What the hell is he going to know about life and
what is going on in our marriage?*

Even at thirty-five, Harold looked like he was in his late
twenties, as if he'd just walked off the beach with a surfboard under

his arm. His eyes were a piercing blue, and he looked as if he'd just shaken the sand from his hair.

"Do you trust your husband with credit cards or your family checkbook and finances?"

"No," I answered.

"Do you trust your husband when he calls you and tells you where he is or who he is with?"

"No, I don't."

"Do you trust your husband alone, when you are not around or out of town?"

"No."

"Do you trust your husband to watch out for your kids when you are not around?"

"No."

"Do you think your husband has cheated on you?"

"No."

"Are you happy with the way things are going in your marriage?"

"No."

The questions went on for a while, and the number of times that I said "no" over the next few moments started to echo in my mind. Later, Harold's questions lingered in my head when Ben and I went to dinner. We waited for a table at a restaurant called Collector's Café.

"I'm glad this is your problem and not mine. I'd be fine never seeing that guy again," I said to Ben about Harold. Little did I know that many, many sessions were ahead for both of us.

At Ben's next session, Harold dropped a bomb on him. He said Ben had to leave town immediately and enter strict in-patient treatment. He said Ben was out of control and needed immediate, serious help. He didn't even want Ben to return home to pack his bags. He said he'd prefer me to drop a bag of essentials by the office. He wanted to put Ben on a plane that night! Yikes, I thought to myself, this sounded really drastic. But Harold was the expert, and he felt it was necessary. At the time, I didn't know everything Ben and Harold knew.

Harold had recommended that Ben attend Sierra Tucson for his in-patient treatment, but after doing some research on his own,

Ben instead chose the Menninger Clinic in Topeka, Kansas. Ben later told me that he knew the time had come. The jig was up, and Harold helped him see that he needed help.

A few days later, I put Ben on a plane to Kansas, not knowing what was going to happen next. He packed for a two week stay. We thought that was how long it would take to figure out what was wrong with him, then he could come back home and work on himself here in town. I immediately began avoiding people and friends as much as possible, as I would be asked the inevitable question, "Where is Ben?" I told everyone he was in Connecticut to spend time with his sister. I settled in with the kids and waited to hear from Ben.

Chapter Two. The Disclosure

❧☙

August 3, 1997

…This is not fun. My life is on hold while B. reckons
with his demons. I am filled with self-doubt and guilt
about him going away. Have been through so much
this week with B. being away in Kansas. Trying to
keep up with his absence to everyone is very hard so
I try and avoid everyone and don't answer the phone.
Haven't even told my parents and siblings. I am really
hopeful and pray that Ben is seeing how incredibly
destructive he has been to himself and us. The kids
are fine but I know they miss him. Ella came home
from camp yesterday. She grew taller. She seemed
depressed when she came back to the house. I think
it is because B. is away—she denies it. I have been
having good runs since B. has been gone.

One of the first nights that Ben called me from rehab, he asked
me to read a book called *Out Of the Shadows*, by Dr. Patrick Carnes. I
read it and was absolutely shocked. It was a book about sex addiction.
I had never heard about such a thing. I couldn't imagine why he
wanted me to read about something so dark and sick. I called my
brother David.

My younger brother lives in New York City, and he has for
quite a while. He is a documentary filmmaker and college recruiter for
a major university, and he happens to be gay. I vaguely remember the
day he came out to me, telling me he was more attracted to men than
women, that he was pretty sure he was gay. I can remember having
my suspicions but dismissing them because of his popularity with
girls in high school. He even dated girls in college. Girls loved him.

When someone finally comes out and admits something like that, it is a bit like dropping a bomb.

For my sisters and me, it wasn't a bomb at all, just a firecracker. It almost felt like we had known all along. For our father, however, it was an atom bomb.

David came down from New York to tell my parents that he was gay. This must have been the summer of 1986. After pretending and giving excuses for such a long time as to why he didn't have a serious girlfriend to bring to family functions, he finally was in a relationship that he really valued. David was simply tired of living a lie to those who mattered the most to him.

The bomb, then the fallout and concussion of the announcement to our parents, rattled the house. My father was old fashioned and religious. He was not the type to quote a particular Bible verse to a specific situation, but he knew what he believed to be right and wrong. Faced with the thought that his only son was, in his mind, no longer a man, Dad absolutely exploded.

"It's disgusting. It's a sin!" he bellowed from all around the house. His tirade lasted nearly half an hour—this full-throated appraisal of sinning and homosexuality, and most important to him, the "death" of his son. David suddenly no longer existed to my father.

In a rage, he ripped pictures of David from the walls, stomped around the house hollering about not having a son, about men having sex with other men. My mother had no idea what to do, so she and my brother sat at the kitchen table in stunned silence.

It was absolutely awful.

My mother, who usually deferred to my father in moments of decision or strife, said nothing. When he continued removing photos from the walls of the house, David had had enough, and he walked out the front door.

Their relationship never rebounded. My brother had been the apple of our father's eye, the sole heir to carry on the family bloodline. After that night, the only thing my father could see was an abomination and a sinner.

My father kept good on his promise of disowning David. We would talk about David when we were all together but nothing more than information of the week and quick updates. As soon as my father entered the room and realized the topic of conversation, he would try and silence us, as if information about my brother, his only son, physically hurt his ears.

I called my brother the night before Ben was scheduled to contact me, after I read *Out of the Shadows*. I picked my brother and not my sisters because I remembered once David telling me he had some friends in recovery, and I thought he might have heard of this addiction.

"Why do you think he wanted me to read about that? Have you ever heard of such an addiction?" I asked David.

"Yeah, I've heard of it," he said.

"Listen to this," I told him. Then I read David excerpts I had marked with a yellow highlighter. "There are three levels of sexual addiction divided by behaviors, legal consequences, and victims."

I continued reading. "Level one is masturbation, compulsive relationships, pornography, prostitution, strip clubs, and anonymous sex with women, men and both men and women."

"Level two deals with exhibitionism, voyeurism, indecent phone calls, and indecent liberties, whatever that means. There is no way he is doing anything in level three."

"It's probably just level one, the masturbation thing," David said. "I wouldn't worry about it too much. Call me after you talk to him and let me know what is going on."

I immediately felt better when he said that. "I guess I'll find out tomorrow night when I talk to Ben," I told him.

After I hung up with David, I thought back and the only thing I could connect to Ben in the realm of sexual deviance were a few occasions of masturbation. OK. I think I can deal with that. Immediately, I could recall instances of him and his friends making jokes and references to masturbation. But what did I know? I'd even caught Ben a few times in the middle of "pleasuring himself," as he liked to call it, and even then I'd thought it simply embarrassing and nothing else. I certainly did not view it as a "dangerous addictive behavior."

About a week and a half into his treatment program, my husband called me around 10:30 at night. Our kids were in the living room a few yards away from my closed bedroom door, watching a movie. At that time, Ella was tall and thin at twelve, Henry was ten, Harper was nine and still wearing her gymnastics leotard from practice that night, and little Olivia was just six.

I can still remember looking at the phone as it rang the first long and full ring. It looked like a foreign object, and the noise it was making was an intrusion. I wanted to pick it up, and I didn't want to pick it up. After the second ring, I reached for the receiver.

"Hello?"

"Hi," Ben said on the other end. He sounded tense and got straight to the point.

"Hi, honey," I said, trying to keep my voice level and normal. "How's your week going?"

"I am doing all right. Did you read the book I asked you to read? The Carnes book?"

"I did read it," I said. "So, what level are you?" I had meant it to be a light, almost comical question, as a way to ease the tension.

"The first," he said.

A wave of relief flowed over my shoulders and back. A chronic masturbator, while a little off-putting and gross, is still manageable. That's not so bad, I thought.

"I figured," I told him, then asked, "Well? What part of level one are we talking about?"

"At one time or another, almost all of it."

This was not a good list to be on. This was the prostitution, pornography, anonymous sex list.

"Almost all of it?" I asked. I felt like I'd been kicked in the stomach. I doubled over at my waist.

"Yeah, almost all of it," he said. He went on to tell me that he had also abused drugs and alcohol, but the sexual addiction was full blown, the true addiction in his life. He said that he had been a sex addict way before we ever married—that this disease had started in his early teens. His disease had flourished during our fourteen-year marriage. He then said I needed to get tested for sexually-communicable diseases, most importantly HIV. My beloved husband had been having anonymous, faceless, unprotected sex even while I was pregnant with our children.

I dropped the phone.

I fell to my knees.

For a few moments, I had the sensation of falling down a deep, dark hole. I believe now that I fell into hell on earth. I think I went into shock. My breath got shorter and shorter, and I began to hyperventilate. With every quick exhale, I quietly, almost in a whisper, repeated the words, "God, what am I going to do?"

Still on the floor, I rocked slightly back and forth. I could hear Ben weeping on the phone from where the receiver lay next to me. He kept saying, as if he were answering me, "I don't know, I just don't know." I reached for the phone, a white Slim line, and I hung up the receiver.

I realized that night, that the one person who I should have been able to count on—to guard my heart, my very life—didn't exist and never had for my entire married life. I had an overwhelming feeling of being utterly alone on this Earth.

As soon as I caught my breath enough to cry, I wept deep, long sobs that came from within my soul. I was physically sick with disbelief over his behavior. My life was a total, complete lie.

The kids were in the living room waiting for me to say good night and put them to bed. They may very well have saved my sanity that night.

I pulled myself together and opened my bedroom door. Thankfully, the only light on was from the TV, so the kids couldn't see my red and swollen eyes. I asked if any of them wanted to sleep with me that night. That wasn't a common occurrence, but I needed the reassurance of my children, pure and real, next to me. Two of the kids, including Harper, jumped at the chance and got into our bed. The other two slept peacefully in their own rooms, not knowing what had just happened between their parents.

I kept the TV on all night. I must have dozed off and on that night. The phone rang around 2 a.m. The caller was Sally, one of Ben's therapists from Menninger. She said Ben had called her and told her what he had disclosed to me over the phone. Everyone at Menninger had asked him not to do that over the phone. She said she was sorry he had. They wanted him to wait until I was there with him.

"How are you feeling?" Sally asked.

"How do you think I am feeling?" I said, my voice was flat and emotionless.

She started to give me some pat therapy jargon—bullshit—and I cut her off.

"I can't go into this right now," I said. "I have two small children sleeping beside me."

She suggested I call Menninger first thing in the morning to plan an immediate trip to Kansas, so I could meet with Ben and his doctor. Then Ben's therapist said something I'll never forget, something I now say to other people in crisis.

"We certainly understand if you don't want to deal with this and just decide to divorce Ben immediately," she said. "A lot of people do that. However, if at all possible, I would encourage you not to make such a major, life-changing decision when you are in the midst of such severe emotional distress. If at all possible, Maurita, come out here, learn about your husband's addiction, take the time to work through some of your extreme emotions before you decide what to do with your marriage."

It was one of the most important things anyone had every said to me in my life. It made sense.

This next journal entry is what I wrote after my husband's disclosure. It reflects the first few days of me trying to wrap my brain around what I had just found out about Ben and his double life.

August 8, 1997

…Had a good day today blocking everything out until about 5 p.m. What I found out about B's behavior before and during our entire relationship and marriage is just too much to take in at once. After finding out two nights earlier about all his sick fucking fucks—all the hundreds of lies and manipulations—my whole

married life to this point has been a fraud and a
hideous joke. I just can't take it all in at once, because
it is too much for me to bear. I hate him. I want him
to feel what it is like to give so much of yourself to
someone and have it mean nothing. I am going out on
Tuesday to meet with his main therapist Sally (what a
weird voice she has) and some guy named Dr. Richard
Irons to learn more about his "fucking disease." I
am filled with fear, rage, and hopelessness. I have to
accept the fact that I allowed a stupid, selfish pig of
a male (he does not deserve to be called a man) walk
all over me and humiliate me in public and private.
He didn't protect my beautiful kids or me. I will now
call them "my kids" because the selfish pig doesn't
deserve them. I hate him.

I flew out to Kansas a few days later. Since my husband's
disclosure, I had the feeling of living in a continuous nightmare,
except I was walking around and functioning like a regular human
being. I felt like a freak, a fraud, someone who was no longer of this
earth. Every moment of my life became drenched with indecision
and self-doubt.

At the rental car counter in Topeka, for example, the attendant
asked me an innocent, benign question.

"Is this business or pleasure?" he asked.

I thought to myself, *How could I possibly answer what this trip is
for, what this means for my life, my children's lives?* Nothing about my life
felt normal anymore and wouldn't for years to come.

During the drive to the hotel where Ben was staying, my heart
was pounding. He was allowed to live off the grounds of the treatment
center after it was determined he was clean and sober and not a danger
to himself. I honestly didn't know how I would react to seeing him for
the first time.

Suddenly, I found myself caught in a horrible, dark thunder
and lightning storm. The storm grew so dangerous so quickly that I
had to pull off the interstate under a bridge and sit out the torrential

downpour. I leaned over and rested my forehead on the steering wheel and cried my eyes out.

Grief and fear of the unknown became my new, constant companions.

I eventually arrived at his motel and went up to his room and knocked on the door. The rain was down to a drizzle as he opened the door. We just looked at each other for a moment and then we hugged each other. I cried and he wept. We didn't really talk much that first night—we were like strangers and very careful with what we said to each other.

The next day I met with Ben's treatment team. He had a main physician, Dr. Richard Irons, plus a couple of different therapists who specialized in different areas of treatment. I'd been told to wear long pants and shirts with long sleeves that did not reveal much skin. They wanted Ben to be in a zero stimulation environment.

We sat down in Dr. Irons' office along with his primary therapist, Sally. Ben was sitting beside me—a big gap between us, drinking a cup of coffee and staring down at the floor. Dr. Irons and Sally sat directly in front of me.

Before going to Menninger I had already decided that if he had not raped anyone or touched a child in an inappropriate way, I would at least stay with him until he completed any suggested in-patient treatment. Now, here I sat listening to an introductory course on sex addiction and how it relates to men in general and Ben specifically.

Ben buried his face in his hands. Every once and a while, I looked over at him and his face was gray with anguish at what was being said. The truth about how he had been living his life was finally out in the light of day.

At Sally and Dr. Iron's urging, I asked Ben a couple of questions.

"Ben," I said slowly, "have you ever raped anyone?"

"No," he said quietly.

"Have you ever molested anyone?"

"No."

"Have you ever inappropriately touched a child?" Then, I asked, "Our children?"

The gravity of that question hit my husband hard. He looked over at me, horrified, that I would even think to ask that and said, "No, absolutely not."

After a few moments , I looked at Dr. Irons.

"OK, Dr. Irons, I will stay and hear what he has to say."

"Thank you, Maurita," Dr. Irons said.

Because of Ben's fear of my reaction and extreme shame in telling me about his double life, he could barely look me in the eye. It was Dr. Irons who summarized the bulk of Ben's sexual behavior and told it to me in a professional yet "matter of fact" way. Because of Dr. Iron's demeanor, I was strangely calm as we began the session. Still, there was no softening the meaning behind the words.

"Ben has had, over the course of your relationship and marriage, over a hundred extramarital sexual encounters," explained Dr. Irons. "Some men in their addiction have to take on higher levels of risk to receive the desired feelings of reward. They build up a tolerance, if you will. Ben was always after the next high, the next thrill. The thrill of taboo sex, like prostitutes and strippers, was a tremendous high for him. Both of you will need to undergo HIV tests every three months to permanently rule out infection."

I was horrified. I immediately thought I had AIDS. It would eventually take me almost ten months to get tested, I was so afraid. I thought people would say, "Why is Ben's wife coming in for blood work? He must have cheated on her." I was mortified. My mouth was too dry to verbalize it right then, but I think my face went a shade lighter as Dr. Irons continued to speak.

I thought, *What about the kids? Do we have to get the kids tested, too?*

Dr. Irons continued to divulge some of the scattered and sordid details of Ben's sexual compulsions. Ben's conscious exploits manifested during his time in Grenada at medical school. There seemed to be a forever steady infusion of tourists going to the islands who enjoyed several drinks along with anonymous vacation sex.

He said the sex was never personal. Ben did not even know these young women's names. *Oh, great. Is that supposed to make me feel better?* I thought.

Quick, faceless, nameless sexual release was the drug of choice for Ben, but he used other drugs like alcohol, marijuana, and ecstasy to fuel his sexual acting out.

I listened as best I could, but my thoughts were scattered and fragmented. Who did I really marry and where did this behavior come from?

Dr. Irons ended our discussion with more grim news. "Statistically your marriage has a 98 percent chance of failure due to the length of time and scope of Ben's addictive behavior. There is also a 95 percent chance of Ben having a sexual relapse in the first five years of his recovery."

I slumped in my chair at this final blow. I could no longer hear the words of Dr. Irons. I was numb, shocked, and totally overwhelmed by the information and picture that was being painted before me.

"Did you ever think I would find out about any of this?" I asked Ben.

"No."

"Did you ever think you'd get caught?"

"No," he said. "I thought I was in complete control of it all. I thought I was too good at hiding it. Getting caught didn't even occur to me."

I looked at him, not knowing what to say. *What a moron*, I thought to myself.

છ૭૯૩

Part Two: The Desert of Recovery

છ૭૯૩

Chapter Three. My New Reality

꧁꧂

I returned home truly traumatized and broken by what had been going on behind my back. I immediately started seeing Ben's therapist, Harold, on a weekly basis. It soon became apparent I couldn't handle the trauma and grief I was feeling, so I moved to a twice a week schedule.

I had married a man who had been living a double life. He could remember being as young as seven or eight and masturbating. He was strangely attracted to looking at pornography, shown to him by his friendly neighborhood barber. His early teens and high school years were the breeding ground for alcohol abuse and multiple, casual sexual encounters. Casual sex came especially easy during his summers as a lifeguard on the New Jersey Shore.

I was left with the truth about who I had married. My own husband, the father of my children, the man I expected to grow old with, had looked me in the eyes and lied to me hundreds of times. He betrayed me to the depth of my soul.

Ben's in-patient stint at Menninger lasted for more than three months. I felt like a human shield, protecting my family from each inquisitive call or comment. Everyone wanted to know where Ben had been, where he was now, what he was going through.

"He'll be back soon," I'd say with a forced smile. "Better than ever."

I was appalled at this whole situation, how it made me feel, how it made me look. A combination of desire for secrecy and fear of judgment kept my responses curt yet hopeful. I retreated from life as I had known it and hunkered down in my house, Harold's office, or in recovery meetings. I awoke each day with the agony of my husband's double life. I went to bed with this new reality each night, and it was the last thought in my head as I drifted off to a couple of hours sleep.

My sleep pattern changed. I could only sleep a few restless hours a night, and I was plagued with nightmares for the first two or three years of recovery. Ben's betrayal accompanied me no matter what I did. It became a part of me.

To make matters worse, if that were possible, some of Ben's medical colleagues and business associates were suddenly cruel and disrespectful to me in his absence.

One of Harold's first "assignments" for me was to go to Al-Anon, a support group for spouses and family members of alcoholics. I didn't understand why he wanted me to go to this group, as Ben's problem was clearly defined as a sexual addiction. His drinking was not really a problem and hadn't caused me any real agony. I needed to meet with women whose husbands were sex addicts. Unfortunately, no other women in my community had come forward and started any kind of support group. Harold knew Al-Anon would be my only immediate alternative.

"It's for support," he said after a few minutes. "In your mind, just replace the word *alcohol* with *sex addiction*. Allowing yourself to be in an environment of support is a must for you and will be an important part of your recovery process." Harold's voice was always so even tempered. He kept a perpetual poker face on and I couldn't tell what he was thinking or what he'd say next. At times I felt that he could handle and fix anything. He was no nonsense, tough, brutally honest, even relentless sometimes, but he also knew when to back off.

He told me to go to six meetings in a row before I made any decisions about whether I was comfortable with the meeting or the other women.

The building where the meetings were held was only fifteen or twenty minutes away from my house, depending on traffic. It stood alone, a red brick building that, I believe was owned or donated by a recovering alcoholic because it's only use was for Alcoholics Anonymous (A.A.) and Al-Anon meetings.

The interior was not very inviting or comfortable. As a matter of fact, it was downright depressing looking. But the more I went to meetings and began to feel a part of the group, the more the look of the room didn't matter.

The meeting room contained folding chairs and a desk where the chairperson sat and conducted the meetings. There was an ever-present coffee maker on a table in the corner. I learned that the first one to arrive at the meeting got the coffee started. The walls were sparsely decorated with some nicely worded recovery sentiments, and on one wall hung the Twelve Steps and Twelve Traditions of A.A. and Al-Anon. The Steps are:

1.   We admitted we were powerless over alcohol, that our lives had become unmanageable.
2.   Came to believe that a Power greater than ourselves could restore us to sanity.
3.   Made a decision to turn our will and our lives over to the care of God as we understood him.
4.   Made a searching and fearless moral inventory of ourselves.
5.   Admitted to God, to ourselves, and to another human being the exact nature of our wrongs.
6.   Were entirely ready to have God remove all these defects of character.
7.   Humbly asked Him to remove our shortcomings.
8.   Made a list of all persons we had harmed, and became willing to make amends to them all.
9.   Made direct amends to such people wherever possible, except when to do so would injure them or others.
10.   Continued to take personal inventory and when we were wrong promptly admitted it.
11.   Sought through prayer and meditation to improve our conscious contact with God as we understood Him, praying only for knowledge of His will and the power to carry that out.
12.   Having had a spiritual awakening as the result of these steps, we tried to carry this message to others and to practice these principles in all our affairs.

Having never been to any kind of recovery meeting before, I dreaded walking into that door for the first time. I feared what would happen in the meetings, and I feared seeing someone I might recognize. Worse yet, I feared that someone would recognize me.

Luckily for me, my agony was worse than my ego. At my first three meetings all I did was cry. I would walk in, set my diet Coke and my keys on the chair to my left, my books and purse on the chair to my right, and physically cringe if anyone tried to sit near me.

I walked into those Al-Anon meetings a shell of a woman. My heart and spirit were absolutely shattered. The women I met in those few meetings were so kind and compassionate and open. Most of them had been in recovery for a long time, so they had really smart, honest, and inspiring things to say. They allowed me the opportunity to grieve in a respectful and safe environment. One of the things that struck me the most in those first few meetings was that some of the women were actually smiling, some even laughing at their circumstances and loved ones. I remember looking at them in those moments feeling so hopeless and sad. I could not picture myself ever laughing again.

I think I cried every day of my first year in recovery. Sometimes, I cried for a few seconds or a few minutes. Sometimes I cried gut-wrenching sobs. Grief seemed to pour out of me. I grieved the death of who I thought my husband was and what I thought my marriage was. I grieved the death of my dreams for my children and the family legacy they would have to deal with in their futures.

Most of all, I grieved for my broken heart and shattered spirit—both as a woman and as a wife.

I eventually became comfortable with my Al-Anon meetings, and I attended two to three meetings a week for the first three years of my recovery. This group was a vital part of my healing process. Participating in Al-Anon also sparked the beginning of my spiritual recovery. It was the first time I had ever thought about or publicly talked about having an intimate, daily relationship with a Higher Power or the God of my understanding.

My first year in recovery was by far the most painful. I felt tremendous shame over Ben's behavior. I was also ashamed that I had married someone who would do the dark, sick, sex stuff that he was into. It was a year of "putting out fires," as my therapist called it. I had so many raw emotions to deal with that I didn't focus on my own choices and behaviors until well into the second year of my journey.

My family came through for me when I needed them most. Because I was so wounded and shell-shocked in those first few months while Ben was away, just doing everyday things like food shopping was difficult. My parents were wonderful. They came down almost immediately and stayed in our beach house for a week. I didn't have the courage to tell them about the sexual addiction; instead, I told them he was a drug addict. My father, being in the insurance business, did all the leg work to get Ben's disability forms processed. He also gave me sound financial advice and budget suggestions. My mother took care of all the kids' back to school shopping needs. They didn't have the heart to ask much about Ben being away so long, but they were not idiots. I now believe they knew it was a lot worse than drug abuse.

"Have these doctors given you any kind of time frame as to when he'll be able to go back to work? You can't survive on disability checks forever," my father said one day as we finished going through my family finances.

"They really haven't said a specific time," I tried to explain. "It seems like everything is wait and see." Then I felt the tears coming. "I know he will be able to go back to work eventually, but I'd rather not sit around and wait. I want to be proactive and figure out how to manage our finances until he goes back to work."

"Was he stepping out on you and the kids?"

"No," I said, the tears welling behind my eyes. "No, Dad, of course not," I lied. I was too ashamed to admit to my parents that Ben was a sex addict. Plus, I was fearful that my father would make Ben's life miserable, whether we stayed married or not, and would never forgive him for what he did to me if I told him the truth.

My brother David came down from New York City for a week and really helped out with the kids. Ben's cousin Jeff came for five days too. What a blessing because the kids really love my brother and "Uncle Jeff." They thought their uncles' visits were a treat, and I found their presence a source of great relief and emotional support.

My in-laws were a different story. They did come and help out our nanny Lizzie take care of the kids while I went to the mountains of

Maggie Valley for my first therapeutic weekend retreat with Harold. Although I was grateful for their help, it was hard to figure out what to say to them. It was Ben's responsibility to tell his parents what was going on with him—not mine.

They did not understand why he had to be away for three and a half months. At one point, I started to explain that Ben needed to explore his childhood and teenage years to understand his current emotional issues.

"That's bullshit," Helen said as she scoffed at me. "Whatever happened to Ben happened after he left home for college."

It was classic blame-shifting, denial, and mother-in-law logic. If something was wrong with her son it had to be because of the woman he married, not because of her parenting or his childhood. For the most part, Ben's parents were a source of pain and a reminder of the fraud in my life.

I had no choice but to back away from conversations with Helen. Ben's parents never had any knowledge of what was really going on in his life—and probably never would. They certainly didn't need to know the sordid details of his addiction or the intricacies of our lives, so I kept quiet around them and saved the words for my journal.

October 2, 1997

…Walter and Helen finally left yesterday at 5 p.m. They are fucking unbelievable. Walter is in complete denial and checked out, and Helen is overwhelmed and angry. They have no idea how painful some of the things they say to me are. For example, they brought up Ben having an affair. What affair? What are they even talking about? He didn't have an affair! I was so angry that they just assumed he was having a love affair of some sort when I knew that wasn't the case. Then they asked, "Did he have any other children that you're aware of?" Nice. Shove something else in my brain to worry about. They complained the entire time they were here. I fought fear and nausea all day today.

I know better. I know not to worry about things I have
no control over, so why am I doing it? Very depressing.

As far as Ben's business was concerned, Bill, one of Ben's best
friends and our family lawyer, became a rock of support for me. Ben
and Bill started their practices almost at the same time in the same part
of town. They were two boys from New Jersey who made good. Bill
built a thriving law practice. He and his beautiful, smart wife, Laura,
were loving, nonjudgmental friends to Ben and me.

My first meeting with Bill after getting back from seeing Ben in
treatment was really tough. I sat down in his office and began telling
him a little about what Ben's treatment program was like and why he
had to stay out of town and away from his practice for so long. While
we were talking, Bill asked me if I had found out about any infidelity.

I looked at him and said, "Yes." I put my head down and burst
into tears, ashamed and humiliated. When Bill stands up straight,
he is just over six feet tall, and while I imagine him as a serious force
to be reckoned with in the courtroom, I've always known him as
the chuckling chef standing over large vats of spaghetti and Italian
sausage, cooking for his family and friends.

He came around his desk and gave me a big hug. Once
he understood our situation, he advised me to take over power of
attorney for my husband's practice so we could keep everything
running smoothly. Larry, one of the associates, took care of the day-to-
day decisions for the practice, and he did a decent job. Bill also went
over with my Dad any insurance problems, budget, and financial
concerns.

Our plan was to start selling of our assets one by one until
Ben's disability checks kicked in. The first thing I sold was my
husband's two-seater black Mercedes coup. It sold as fast as I could
place an ad in the newspaper.

Watching that small Mercedes pull out of our driveway and
head up the street was strangely empowering. Although I enjoyed
owning such a nice car, the game had changed. My family's financial
survival was at stake, and material things no longer mattered to me.
Doing the right thing and taking responsibility felt right.

Friday, October 24, 1997

Wow, what a day—carpooled kids, went to the office and signed checks. Mike, another of Ben's associates, had Larry and the bookkeeper upset. He came to them at the eleventh hour with a $4,000 malpractice insurance bill he wanted paid immediately. Mike totally blew me off when I told him I was running late and wanted to make an Al-Anon meeting. Said his needs were more important. Arrived at Al-Anon ten minutes late. When it was my turn to read, I started crying. Had no idea I felt so sad; I had no warning. I felt overwhelmingly depressed and hopeless about my life. I am really praying and doing things that I am supposed to be doing, but I feel no peace or comfort, only loss and emptiness. Left Al-Anon and went to Harold's. I feel emotionally down and physically tired. I hate it when he asks me how I am doing because I am always the same—I am broken. Am actually beginning to feel comfortable with Harold. I can say anything to him—he won't be shocked and if he is laughing at me he has the good grace and professionalism not to show it.

Sunday, October 26, 1997

I skipped a fun party Saturday night—stayed home and had an intense call with Ben instead. Blew up at him after listening to him tell me about his mother's comments about me and my mothering style with the kids. Critical commentary from her is galling, to say the least. Then asked B. how he was going to handle his friends when he got home. Got into a fight over that until he hung up on me. I was so angry. Not being able to confront him face to face with my anger and hurt is really hard for me. I don't know how to handle it. He called back 5 min. later. I had calmed down and so had he. We were able to talk things out a little more levelheaded. He threw me for a loop when he questioned why I don't look into seeing a female therapist. What is up with that? He even made a comment about women running away with their therapists. Is he worried about that or just trying to manipulate me and cast doubt on me for trusting Harold more than I trust him? The only thing he should be concerned with is if I think I can be honest with Harold and feel comfortable enough to let him help me with my fucked up marriage. Went to bed at 1 a.m.

Chapter Four. Digging Deeper

℘ℭ

Wednesday, October 29, 1997

…Had a nice conversation with Ben. I mean I was calm and controlled. Harold was tough yesterday. He thinks I am still in a bubble. I have moments when I feel so sure that Ben and I can work everything out. Sometimes I feel such a great love and connection to him that I am sure we can win this battle. Other times, I feel our problems are insurmountable. I have come to the conclusion that only my heart will tell me what to do and what direction to go toward. I must stop asking Harold or anyone, "What would you do in my place?" No one can answer that for me. I am climbing the walls waiting for B's blood test; it's been three months. I really have asked everyday for God to take away my fear and worry about this issue.

I went looking for God the day before Halloween.

I had remembered something my father had always said as we were growing up. He said, "No matter what is going on or where you are in life, you can always find refuge and safety in a church. It will always be a safe harbor for you."

I dropped Olivia and Harper off at school that morning. Feeling anxious and out of sorts, I took my father's advice and drove to St. Michael's to calm down. But I didn't go in because it was right in the middle of morning mass. I needed the solitude and sanctuary of a chapel, not the creaking of the two massive doors followed by the sound of fifty people shifting in their pews to stare at the sad-looking woman walking in late.

I tried St. Andrew's. It was the same thing, middle of mass. I gave up on that idea and ended up at Target, slowly rolling my red cart up and down the aisles, mindlessly looking at clothes and brushed metal picture frames.

God was not at Target. No surprise there.

I was beginning to think that I didn't know how to find God anymore, and that revelation scared me because I knew I would need His help throughout this dark period of my life. I won't give up, I told myself, but feeling lost and no connection with God didn't make it any easier.

Friday night, Oct. 31, 1997, 11:50 p.m.

I am so tired and feel so fucked up emotionally that I need to just outline how my day went today.

> 7:30—Ben's office—stuck dealing with business stuff
> 9:30—Al-Anon—discussed fear
> 11:00—newspaper—to drop off an ad
> 12:00—home
> 1:00—nap
> 2:00—pick up Harper
> 3:00—Jazzy, our dog, has a seizure on the floor
> 4:00—Dad calls, has a spot on his bladder—
>   surgery to follow
> 6:00—Ben calls
> 7:00-10:30—did some painting
> 11:00—shower and eat
> 11:52—finish this journal

"I feel totally out of control, really vulnerable and tired," I told Harold during our usual Tuesday morning sessions. "I feel like I am stepping into something very emotionally deep and serious."

"I think we should explore the possibility of you taking some time for some more in-depth treatment," he said.

"Yeah, sure, Harold. And where do you suppose we come up with more money? Ben isn't even home yet and you want me to go away?"

"I'm not suggesting you leave today," Harold said. "Just eventually. We'll get Ben home and acclimated, and we'll keep doing our own work here, but I think it's something you should start to think about."

When Ben arrived home from Menninger, we both tried to maintain our civility to one another for the sake of the kids and to ease our way into the questions and comments from our friends and other people in the community. We still shared a bedroom, but one of us usually ended sleeping on the couch in the upstairs family room. The hurt and fear I felt toward Ben was so much stronger than any physical urge.

Ben took it upon himself to tell our oldest daughter, Ella, about his infidelity. Moments like that just made my blood boil.

November 15, 1997

…Very angry that he told Ella about his sex outside of marriage. I wish I could staple his mouth shut. She is a child and I hate to think of the weight he just dumped on her shoulders….

I was writing regularly in my journal, especially when something eventful happened, including this night when I fought with Ben.

November 26, 1997

Last Friday, Ben came home from synagogue twenty-five minutes late. In the meantime, Ben's sister called and reminded me, innocently, that my wedding anniversary was the following day. That really stung because I did not give it any thought until she mentioned it. I felt such a sense of loss, sadness, and anger that my wedding day would never be a day to celebrate again, thanks to his behavior.

I verbally attacked Ben the minute he walked in the door. We had agreed that any time he was going to be more than fifteen minutes late, he would call. He did not. Anytime he is so late and doesn't call, my imagination goes to a dark, untrusting place.

Once Ben arrived home, I screamed at him to pack his bags and leave. His responses were quiet until I began to push him in the hallway. He retreated to the pool area. I followed him there and just lost the will to yell anymore, collapsing near the edge of the pool and sobbing.

We went to Harold together the next session and decided that my behavior had been out of control and bordering on physically abusive. I did not disagree.

The holidays were marching toward us one unpleasant day at a time. We had Lizzie, our part-time nanny, on overdrive with the kids. With Ben focused on his treatment and me struggling to keep focused on my own recovery, it felt like a full time job. I was trying to help Ben instead of hurting us both by flying off the handle, but I struggled with my patience and my temper. I was stung and smack-dab in the middle of the anger phase of healing.

I wished Thanksgiving would evaporate.

"I think you should try to be enthusiastic about Thanksgiving and Christmas, Mo," Harold told me. "For yourself, for the kids. There is a lot of good that can come from being together during the holidays."

That first Christmas was even worse. We had little money to spend, I didn't want or expect anything from him, and I didn't buy him anything. I did the bare minimum of decorating for the kids' sake. I think Olivia and maybe Harper still believed in Santa, so I had to swallow my apathetic attitude and decorate the Christmas tree, set up the manger scene, and bake some chocolate chip cookies.

After all the presents were opened, Ben and I went out on the front porch and sat on some chairs and watched Henry play basketball with his new ball and backboard. I was sitting there feeling so empty and sad, intermittently cheering Henry on if he got a basket.

Then Ben turned to me, with no warning and said, "I went through a brief period while I was at Menninger where I thought if my AIDS test came back positive, I would walk out of the treatment center, buy a gun on the way back to Myrtle Beach, lie to you and tell you that I was ok to come home, and then kill you and myself—rather than tell you that you or I had been exposed to the virus."

What? It was another blow to my stomach and the butterflies started their all too familiar dance. I looked at him and said, "You know what? I have no doubt you would have done it." I got up and walked inside the house. I told Harold about that Christmas conversation in my next session, and he was very concerned, documenting everything I said. He called Ben right after I left, and they met immediately so Harold could judge for himself if I was even safe being around Ben.

Ben couldn't help me when the pain began, because mine was different from his. There we were, together, me crying on the bed, and Ben overwhelmed and helpless. So, we defaulted to something familiar, something that had been ripped from our lives. We defaulted to our mundane, old life, to that which made us feel like a normal, married couple, even though we both knew we were not.

I fixed him a Philly cheese steak sandwich. We watched reruns of "Frasier" and paid the bills. The show was hysterical.

During my sessions with Harold, he gave me several writing assignments. These writings were to allow me to vent my emotions in a safe and healthy way. This particular assignment tapped into the white-hot center of the rage that wrapped my life so tightly during the early stages of my recovery. I felt that everything that everyone did around this time was done directly to me, so much so that even Jazzy, our dog, accidentally drinking anti-freeze felt like a malicious, painful attempt to bring down my family and me.

I knew that voicing my resentments was meant to help me release them and see them in the stark light of day. So, I wrote the following letter to Ben and voiced how I felt, no holds barred. This letter was meant for Harold's eyes only. Ben never saw it.

Ben,

I am angry and resentful at you for the following reasons:

How could you have possibly done this to me? I really thought you loved me and the idea of committing to me and taking responsibility for having children and sticking around to make sure they have the things they need to make them loving human beings. You have failed me in so many ways. I honestly don't care what you did before we married. All things changed when you put that ring on my finger—in front of our families, the judge, and God. To think you lied to me even at that time is just so unbelievable. You are weak and gutless. I hate you for the way you twisted all your sick behavior around and threw it back in my face and made me start doubting my sanity and myself. I hate you for leaving me alone so many nights when the kids were babies and sick. You said you were at the hospital, but you really weren't.

I resent the fact that you are seen as the upstanding, great citizen and hardworking Dad and physician to so many people, but you are an addict and a destructive, manipulative shithead to me.

I hate it when you flirt. Your behavior around other women makes me feel ugly, fat, and unworthy. I hate it when I question you in a hostile manner and you retreat and get smug.

I can't believe you were so sick and I didn't realize it. I hate you for putting your kids and me at serious physical risk because of your inability to suppress your sick sexual fucked up addiction.

I resent you for always throwing younger, thinner women in my face. I resent you for not appreciating the woman I have become. I hate you for having to go to Menninger for three months. I resent all the new debts you have incurred. We are going backward, not forward.

I hate you for telling me your addictions over the phone. I resent the fact that I married a man not strong enough to tell me something so incredibly important to my face.

I had to do everything and cover for you. I had to put up a good face as my private world crumbled. I have almost been driven insane by the kids' issues, financial concerns (both personal and business), running the house. I resent the power I have allowed you to have over my life. I resent and feel deeply hurt that you haven't taken better and more loving care of me. You have let me down more than I will ever be able to articulate. Because of you, I trust no one and I believe in nothing. You robbed me of that.

I resent you for hurting and causing anxiety to my parents and my family at a time when they have enough to worry about. I hate myself for loving you and sticking with you and for putting up with it for years.

—Maurita

This letter was an important step for me and my therapy sessions with Harold. We were able to pinpoint and work through, piece by piece, my resentments, anger, and fear.

I noticed that my son, Henry, was having attitude issues. One day he got very upset and said I didn't care about him. "All you do is sit in your room and paint, and you never do anything with me." I clearly saw the hurt on his face as he stomped away. I made him come back, face me, and tell me what he wanted. He said he wanted me to do stuff with him and pay attention to him. I said, "OK." Then we discussed how good it was that he was able to show his feelings and cry. I told him he would always be much healthier for letting his feelings and needs be known, rather than stuffing them inside. I told him that is one of the reasons his dad got so sick and had to go away, because he had no safe way when he was growing up to show his emotions. We gave each other a big hug and a kiss and off he went.

A part of me knew that my children felt ignored by me, but the pain I carried was too heavy. Ben's behavior had broken my heart and torn my spirit into pieces. In addition, Ben was still dealing with a bout of self-consciousness and worrying that I would run off with my therapist. I know that his lack of self-confidence was influencing his thinking. After all, his low self-esteem is what got us into this mess.

"Have you given more thought to the place I recommended in Tucson?" Harold asked during one of our morning sessions. "Did you have a chance to look at that brochure I gave you?"

"I don't know," I told him. "Sounds like a bunch of kooky group therapy." I wasn't sure I wanted to go. I had so many mixed feelings. I feared that if I went away, Ben would relapse and I would blame myself for it. I feared that the children would miss me too much. I feared that I would get to Tucson, look both ways before crossing the street, and run off into the desert to start my own life without Ben or my kids. I worried that I wouldn't be able to blow dry my hair or have a Diet Coke if I wanted. A glass of wine was obviously out of the question. Who the hell knew what the other nuts were showing up for? Part of me had hoped that I would meet a strong woman with whom I could connect, someone who, like me, had a husband who was a sex addict, some female role model who I could look up to and see what the next few years held in store for me.

In February of 1998, I decided that the possible positives outweighed my fears of abandoning my family for a mentally stable and handsome cowboy, that the progress and increase in personal worth would be more valuable than staying at home and resenting Ben.

Harold and Ben were both proud and excited for me to do this, for myself and my family. I think they both knew how much I needed some time away from the house, a home I now equated with a failed marriage to a man I struggled to love.

Ben returned to a modified and shortened work week, which was a major step in his recovery and a major relief in mine. For the first couple of months back, he was working just three days a week for four hours a day, leaving him with ample time to attend meetings, meet with his sponsor, and spend time with the kids. Exercise was off limits completely as it had become a compulsion for him.

His first day back at work was a big day for us. Part of my husband's recovery was to come up with a healthier work schedule. Ben did not return to work right after he came back from rehab. It was advised that he stay home and get acclimated to his lifestyle change before he jumped back in to the pressures of work. I was resentful of this from the start; we had huge financial concerns because of his being away for so long. Now I see the absolute wisdom in this course of treatment. I am so grateful we had a therapist in our corner who really knew how to treat addiction and the many benefits that in-patient treatment can bring to people's lives.

Days later, Ben's six-month HIV test came back negative, and while he appeared to feel superior for doing nothing more than accidentally avoiding a horrible disease, I still told him we would use condoms if we ever had sex again.

My life wasn't a roller coaster anymore; it was something so much worse. Looking back at my journal entries from around that time, I saw elation followed by despair.

February 20, 1998, morning

…Wow. Three pretty good days in a row. All skirmishes with Ben have been minor and we've been able to nip them in the bud. I chaired my first Al-Anon meeting the other day and have been feeling the occasional wave of excitement about going to Tucson. I wonder what kind of kooky roommate I'll have….

February 20, 1998, evening

…I am incredibly bummed out. I hate my house. I hate my life. I hate everything. I hate the fact that I know who won the women's figure skating event before the fucking broadcast. I didn't look away from the evening news fast enough. Right now I feel sad, mad, betrayed, unloved. I have never been loved—totally loved—by anyone. What a sad feeling. Are my expectations too high? Probably. How sad I have to save my own fucking husband's HIV test results. I am a robot. On top of that, our Springer spaniel, Jazzy, finally died of poisoning.

March 11, 1998, afternoon

…Time flies. Ben and I have been really up and down. Mostly down. He has been feeling bad—retreating— has been cold and remote. I am really realizing how deeply I let him control how I feel. I have no power when it comes to detaching from him. We are going through such a wild ride. I wish it would calm down. Very nervous about leaving for Tucson and facing my life. I fear embarrassment and feeling stupid the most, and I dread having to do some stupid ass role-play drama stuff. I think therapists love that goofy shit.

Chapter Five. Real Life Begins in Tucson

ℰℭ

Since learning that my husband was a sex addict, I have had the privilege of participating in the best possible, most innovative therapy. I am extremely grateful for the care and guidance I have received. I have also dedicated untold hours to Bible study and prayer.

Nevertheless, one of my most difficult trials came at my first group therapy workshop in Tucson, Arizona. Attending local Al-Anon meetings twice a week and private counseling sessions with a familiar therapist had become fairly routine practices for me. Flying out West to be in a more in-depth therapeutic setting with strangers was quite another step. At the same time, it was one of the first times during my recovery that I began to feel like a whole person, who could stand on her own two feet, declare her rights as a human being, and be someone other than Ben's wife.

I was fearful of being on my own, of being so ultimately exposed and vulnerable in front of complete strangers in a strange place. My diligence to stay at the Odyssey workshop came from a place of inner strength that I didn't know existed. It was like finding a brand new room in your house filled with the things that you've been looking for but couldn't find.

My week in Tucson, Arizona, remains one of the most defining periods of my life. I truly participated in intimate, meaningful relationships. I finally understood the value of being honest with yourself, the value of other people's experiences, and the value of forgetting about your own problems and focusing on others.

My adult, emotional life began in Tucson.

I didn't want to go. And when I got there, I didn't want to stay. However, by the fifth and last day, I did not want to leave. In the late 1990s, when I began my recovery, I constantly struggled to find confidants who were going through the same things I was going through. There just wasn't the public knowledge and awareness into sexual addiction and what it does to spouses, loved ones, and family members. I'm not a pioneer and I'm not a psychotherapist. I'm not you. I'm just a woman who has really been through it. The following pages from my first, serious journal reflect some of the hardest and easiest, best and worst days of my life.

March 15, 1998. Atlanta

...On my way to Tucson. Very apprehensive. Gulped down a glass of wine on the plane, so it has taken the edge off, a little. I hate to fly. Ben drove me to the airport in Florence, SC. My eyes can barely stay open and it is only 9:30 p.m. I have to go to the bathroom. Should I go through first class or not? Fuck it—I am not waiting and walking to the back of the plane. I will write when I get to the place I am going. I don't even know the real name of it....

I arrived late Sunday night in Tucson. It was rainy and I was tired and nervous. I got my bags and decided to take a cab. Waited in the airport about twenty minutes until a driver showed up. He was a nice enough guy and turned out to have been a patient himself at Cottonwood a couple of years ago.

We drove in at about 11:00 p.m., and I had no idea where to check in. I really wanted someone there to greet me but there wasn't. I saw a light on in one of the offices. I walked in and found myself facing a bunch of people getting their blood pressure checked by a mean-looking nurse and getting their evening "meds." *What the hell is this?* I thought to myself. My heart was in my throat, and at that moment, I hated Harold.

There was a young guy with dreadlocks who scared me. A minute or two later, one of the nurses dispensing the drugs told me to wait a few minutes and he'd show me where to go.

My little home for the next week would be down the road from the main buildings of Cottonwood Treatment Center, in a private single family home called Odyssey.

The driver was nice enough to wait until I knew where I was supposed to be. He helped me with my bags and finally left. A sliding glass door was open, so I walked in and found my name along with my roommate's name: Mary. I tried to be quiet as I moved my bags in but I woke Mary up anyway. She poked her head up from under her covers and I thought she looked mad. I was so tired I didn't give a shit. We spoke briefly and then I got washed up and went to bed. The fatigue was incredible.

Monday

I woke up nervous. I re-introduced myself to Mary, who introduced herself as "The Queen of Codependency." I went to breakfast with her over at the cafeteria and met the others in the group—we ate in an uncomfortable silence. We all went into the main room together and waited for a few minutes until Joe, the director of the program came in, all big and dressed up. I gave him my check, and then he gave me some information about the program. He looked and sounded sincere, but I got the impression that he really didn't give a shit about us.

I was incredibly uncomfortable. We went into a room with two large windows and a red brick wall at the end of the room. It was filled with overstuffed cushions and a bunch of office chairs. We all sat in the chairs in a close circle and stared at each other and the floor. I don't think any of us knew what we were in for.

Our therapist for the week, a pretty, earthy-looking woman named Nan walked into the room and introduced herself and her background.

Our first order of business was to introduce ourselves and discuss why we had come to Odyssey. When it was my turn, I burst into tears talking about Ben and his disclosure. I had lived my married life in a big bubble of lies. That was a really big deal for me, because I hadn't felt safe enough to tell anyone in my life—except Harold—what had really happened.

What a sense of relief! I felt Nan knew it was an important thing for me to say out loud. As we filed out of the room, Kevin, a group member, put his arm around me for a moment and said, "Wow, Maurita, that was some big fucking bubble." He was so right.

We all went to lunch as a group. Lunch was filled with long, uncomfortable silences and dormitory-like food. The Odyssey therapists had a deal with Cottonwood Treatment Center that our small group could eat meals in their cafeteria, down the street from our house, but we were not allowed to speak to the patients.

During the afternoon session, we drew pictures of our childhoods and where we are now in terms of how we feel about our lives today. In my first picture, representing my childhood, I was happy, climbing trees. In my second picture, I was split in two. One half was all phony and walking around like everything was fine; the other half was heavy with clouds, depression, and storms.

We all filed out to dinner, and I was in a really bad place. I could barely eat anything and fought back tears the entire dinner. I really wanted to just give up, to leave. I had an overwhelming feeling of homesickness. I wanted to call Ben and have him wrap his arms around me even though he made me so angry sometimes. I wanted to see the kids, the dogs.

I was also proud of myself because at that moment, instead of isolating myself, I stuck with everyone. We decided to go for a group walk up the highway and into a little canyon. Almost all the way up the road I was weepy and fighting back tears, barely speaking. I was feeling so scared and alone, and I realized I didn't have anything to hide behind: no music, TV, wine, or stupid People magazines.

I felt lost. I began to see how out of touch I had become; I was empty, fearful, and sadly unfamiliar with establishing relationships outside of my role as the wife of Ben.

I had to force myself to participate in conversations with the group. I distinctly remember the man named Bruce, a tall and attractive Arizona native. Walking back down the canyon that night, Bruce and I fell back a little from the group and I told him about some of our bad investments and my disturbing encounters with some bankers in town during Ben's rehab days. He totally related to my experiences, because he was in the financial business. I felt so much more centered and calm after that walk.

Mary and I stayed up talking a little more and then went to bed. I didn't sleep well and did not dream at all. The blasted heater was too loud, and the room was way too hot.

Tuesday

I woke up early and felt incredibly tired. I looked like shit. We all went to breakfast together. Sitting there with everyone was awkward. I noticed a serious decrease in my appetite. Group therapy started around 9 a.m. Kim went first to explain her drawings. Kim was around my age, had short blonde hair, and didn't look happy. She was quiet and serious, but, oh my God, what a story.

Kim's drawings of herself in a cage were disturbing and dark. After she described her pictures to us, Nan asked her to whom she wanted to "talk." The idea was to direct "conversations" at people who had harmed or hurt her; other members of the group were asked to role play the people to whom Kim would talk. Kim wanted to address her mother, father, brother, and ex-husband.

Kim picked William, a late thirty-something slender British man, to be her father; Kevin, a young snowboarder from Colorado, to be her asshole brother; and me to be her mother. We first had to replay the scene where her dickhead brother tied her up and placed her in a ditch in the back yard and buried her. Nan told me to stand in a corner of the room and shout at Kim (as her mother), "You ruined my life!"

Other group members were instructed to yell similar things; the intent was to recreate Kim's childhood environment. Kim was gripped with fear, pain, and anger. As she tapped into her childhood fear, I was absolutely overwhelmed. I have never seen or been a part of anything like that in my life.

What an incredible scene. I was really thrown by how screwed up and painful her childhood was and how she acted out in front of us —total strangers.

I felt like a spoiled brat, compared to what she had faced. I admired her at that moment because all she cared about was confronting her demons and she didn't give a damn about any of us. What strength she possessed.

Watching Kim's childhood drama come to life was exhausting. I had never been subjected to something so serious and life-altering. Welcome to the human race, Maurita!

At lunch I felt better, and we talked a little more. I was preoccupied, however, because I would have to describe my pictures also. Truthfully, I was scared shitless. We did more role playing after lunch. In one situation, I played the wife of a man in our group. At one point he held my hands, looked in my eyes, and said how sorry he was for his behavior and how much he loved his kids. It was a powerful moment for me, because it was everything I wanted Ben to say to me. Over the course of the day, the emotional revelations of the group drew us into a tight circle of care, compassion, and understanding.

Later that evening several of us met up in the kitchen, and we had ice cream and apple pie together. We talked and laughed, recognizing the camaraderie that was developing among us. The evening ended around 11 p.m. As were getting ready for bed, Mary looked at me with a serious face.

"I don't know why we are laughing so hard tonight," she said.

"Why?"

"There isn't a kernel of humor about our lives right now."

She was right.

We both cracked up laughing. And then we went to bed.

Wednesday

I was full of anxiety because I knew it was my turn to do role-playing. I did not sleep well. I decided the things I wanted to "dump" dealt largely with the hurt I felt toward my father for never paying attention to me. I also wanted to explore my anger at my mother for her lack of support of me. I never felt a connection with her; it seemed that to her, I was a "something to do," instead of a "someone to love." She seemed to have an old-fashioned mentality that the woman keeps the house, and the children are raised to go off and "marry well."

When we started group, Mary played my father and Kim played my mother. I felt good about these pairings as I couldn't relate as easily to Kim and it would be easier to unload.

I sobbed and sobbed as I let my father know how hurt and insignificant I felt when he ignored me and seemed to take our brother, David, everywhere with him. I told him that I was angry that he never expected or demanded anything from me, that he never pushed me.

One particular childhood memory came to the forefront. My siblings and I were young children when President Kennedy was assassinated. I was kneeling down in the library of our home, watching the funeral. My sister had done something funny, I can't remember what, but when I giggled my father leaned over and slapped me across the face so hard that I fell over. I was humiliated and shocked. As I was rehashing this story, I sobbed like the six-year-old girl that I had been. I can still remember seeing my crying face reflected in the black and white television. I can't even imagine striking out at my little Olivia like that.

To my mother, I questioned why she was so unsupportive and never seemed to take an interest in me beyond the basics of life. It seemed as though she was constantly yelling and saying cruel things. She'd pull my hair, wash my mouth out with soap, and even slap me across the face for something I said. I felt worthless and horrible after those episodes. I allowed my parents to slowly break down my spirit, and little did I know I would someday allow my own husband to finish me off.

I ended the Mother/Father role playing by wanting a better relationship with both of them, and I wanted my father to look me in the eye and tell me he loved me. The therapist, Nan, allowed Mary to play that out but cautioned me that I may never hear that from him in this lifetime. It was very emotional but really freeing. The experience gave me a sense of how to begin forgiving them both, and I began to see how to put some closure on my childhood. After that experience, I felt lighter and less angry.

Because of Bruce's physical presence and similar demeanor, he was a perfect choice to play Ben in the next round of role-play.

I sat cross-legged across from him, and Nan put two big pillows between us. I couldn't believe it, but as I started talking and crying I actually felt like I was talking to Ben. I whipped out the photos of the kids that I brought with me and went through, one by one, describing how his behavior and addiction had hurt these children that God had seen fit to create and entrust to us.

I talked about how ripped off, betrayed, humiliated, and defeated I felt. He had chipped away at my spirit by constantly commenting on other beautiful women, pointing out my flaws in front of our friends or family, or directing sarcastic barbs toward me.

Then Nan got a big square cushion, put it between Bruce and me, and she handed me a whiffle bat. Boy, did I just go crazy.

Nan would say something that would trigger something inside of me and I would start screaming, crying, and smashing that bat down on the cushion. All the while, Bruce was standing across from me holding the cushion in place, tears in his eyes from the volume and content of my screaming. After a couple of minutes of doing this, I collapsed, sobbing on the floor. Nan came over and put her arm around me. I couldn't believe I did it! This role-playing stuff worked. I had a great sense of relief.

The group gave their feedback. I listened but had such an absolute emotional rush that I couldn't focus for long. Bruce wept when he gave his feedback; he was at the same place with his wife, for different reasons. Everyone was supportive and proud that I had broken through and examined my pain about Ben.

I felt almost stoned. I felt a sense of peace emanating from where I'd been keeping all the anger, doubt, and sadness. Now I know what that saying, *high on life*, really means.

We broke for dinner and then we all met for an exhibition of sand painting in the big room by the kitchen. I was so emotionally spent from the day's experience that I laid down on some oversized pillows in one corner and dozed off a bit. I could hear the sand painter, who had a calm, soothing voice, talking about his own recovery and life experiences. I remember feeling so protected, safe, and content.

As the sand painting guy was leaving he walked up to me and looked into my eyes.

"Would you mind if I hugged you?"

"No, I guess not," I said. What is it with all these recovery people? Everyone always wants to hug everyone else. He gave me a nice big hug, and it felt natural, good even.

We walked out to the pool and talked and laughed until midnight. I really didn't want the night to end. My day of catharsis was already over.

Thursday

Thursday would be another day of group therapy. After group was done for the day, Bruce took us all out to dinner at an authentic Mexican restaurant. It was hilarious, all of us "inmates" out for the evening. I sat between Kevin and William. A Mariachi band wandered around the restaurant, and the air was filled with rich Mexican music

After dinner, we socialized a little, talking about good times and bad. We eventually filtered off to bed. A wave of sadness came over me. I was the one who hadn't unpacked completely in case I needed to make a fast getaway; I had arrived last, but now I didn't want to leave.

Friday

I didn't sleep well the night before. I am full of anxiety about our last day. I feel so free, so content, so much less angry. We went to breakfast together and later we met in the big room before starting group.

We were getting ready to say our final words to each other, our statements about how the therapy had affected us and how we hoped it would keep working. Kim gave us all bear root and baking soda that had been blessed by a medicine man. Nan had us listen to some great music and gave us all an Apache tear, which is a small, black stone. I cried when I spoke. I don't remember what I said.

Bruce went around the circle and said how each person affected him. When he got to me, he paused, tears starting to run down his face.

"Maurita," he said, "You break my heart. I have felt so many of the things you have felt and told you things I have never told anyone before. I'm so sorry, and I hope that things work out for you and your family, I sincerely do."

Kevin was sweet. He looked at me and said that I embody the kind of woman he wants to marry. My femininity, sense of humor, and sense of commitment are things in me he said he treasures. I felt ten feet tall when he finished. His words meant a lot to me after he had seen me blubbering like a baby over my shortcomings and innermost feelings.

We discussed ways to bring what we have learned about ourselves home with us. Nan wanted me to examine the way in which I use music, TV, wine, shopping, and painting as ways of escaping from my life. Oh, joy. I knew I would have to go head to head about these issues with Harold later.

We all stood and held hands. A few of us said a prayer out loud, someone gave a short speech about friendship and trust. Each of my hands was held tightly by a member of the group. Then we went outside and took pictures. I used up two rolls of film.

Some of us went into town and we went into Barnes and Noble. I bought the new sex addiction book by Dr. Carnes. After all the work I'd been doing that week, I thought it was time I took another long, hard look at this stuff. After I joined everyone at the table in the café, I showed them the book. I suddenly burst into tears, put my sunglasses on, and left the café to sit outside. Kevin followed me outside and William soon followed. The three of us sat there on the curb without speaking, but I greatly appreciated their presence.

Mary and I ended the evening by me telling her the story behind my brother and father's relationship. She had tears in her eyes as I talked about it. She is the epitome of a loving, strong, sincere woman. *I want to be like her when I grow up*, I thought to myself.

Saturday

It was sad to see everyone getting dressed up, putting on make up on, and preparing to go back to their lives. Why was I the only one who didn't want to go back? Mine certainly wasn't the worst story, and yet I was the only one resisting the return home.

When I hugged Kim goodbye, I was weeping again. I would probably never see this woman again, yet she knew so much about me —more than my own husband and family knew. I had developed such deep admiration for Kim because she has extraordinary strength and guts. She seemed to brighten up as the week wore on, and she had a nice smile on her face that last day.

Mary drove me to the Conquistador Hotel and we stood there near the front entrance, not sure what to say to one another. I had a huge lump in my throat. People came and went through the front door as we said our good-byes, often sobbing the words into each others' shoulders. I waved good-bye as she drove away. I picked up my room key, dropped my luggage on the bed, and went straight to the pool with my CD player and my journal. I tried to call the kids, Harold, and Ben, but only got message machines. I felt so disconnected from Harold when I couldn't check in with him.

Eventually, Harold did call me back, and he and I both agreed that maybe I didn't need a whole week in Tucson by myself. Still, I did deserve this time of doing absolutely nothing—to think only of myself.

Sunday

The sky was so blue, I decided to call it Colorado Blue; it reminded me of afternoons in Boulder during college. I spent most of the day at the pool again, and as I was sitting there, a young woman and her son sat a couple chairs away. We chatted a little and when she asked why I was there, I figured I would try to continue to be honest with myself and others. After a few minutes of hearing my story she told me that her husband is a recovering alcoholic and addict who had spent time at Betty Ford.

We talked for two hours and told each other about our marriages. She was in her tenth year of recovery with her husband. Not only have they survived, but they were in a better place than they ever dreamed possible.

"You are where you are supposed to be," Harold sometimes said in our sessions, and until my chance meeting with that woman, I thought that was a phony baloney saying. I changed my mind that day. I began to write in my journal.

>...I have been feeling scared and confused about Ben.
>I am thinking that the closeness we once shared was

not nearly the caliber of closeness I have felt over the last week with the men and women at Odyssey. I am scared shitless about going home.

The question is, Can I find that closeness with Ben? A sick side of me wants to leave my marriage and my children and make a fresh start. I don't feel connected to anyone in Myrtle Beach, except Harold, and he really doesn't count. What if Ben and I can't connect with each other the way I now want us to? I fear I will never be able to trust him again. I am enjoying being on my own, and I want to be in control of my own life. I don't want to leave Tucson, this new, safe place, but I know I have to "grow up and face my responsibilities," as Harold says.

"What do you want?" Harold once asked me.

I want to raise my children and send them into the world as smart and loving and well-equipped to stand on their own two feet. I really want Ben there by my side. I want us to grow old together. But I want to feel completely loved, no matter what I look like on the outside.

Chapter Six. Going Home

ഔ

As I gathered my things in Tucson, sad to see such an emotionally profound week come to a close, I thought of our little beach house and pictured waving sea oats and small dunes in our backyard. It will be good to see the ocean again. Ben would say he likes me better at the beach house, where I am more relaxed, not worrying about day-to-day events in our lives. Our biggest decision at the beach, up to this point, has been what to have for dinner. Now, that's all changed.

On my last day in Tucson, I wrote a final passage in my journal.

March 25, 1998

Oh, brother, my last day in Tucson. I can't believe this has come to an end. It is so beautiful here—breezy, dry and cool. My day began with a wake-up call from Harold. He wanted to know when I was coming back. Told him I was coming home late tomorrow night. I am already panicked about leaving. I hate the thought of flying, and I am nervous about being around Ben.

I had another great day today. Got up early and went to the 4th Avenue street fair. Took a cab and met Bob, a cab driver/recovering sex addict/heroin addict. He called me "a babe and a half." After filling him in on why I was out west, he told me to consult a lawyer and dump Ben. Pretty much everywhere I went I seemed to connect with people—including a young girl at an outdoor café on 4th Avenue and an artist on Congress Street where I bought something. Because my self-esteem has risen a couple of notches I seem to be willing to take more chances with people. I feel like a different person. I bought a $10 leather pouch with beads on it from a guy in a junk shop. It is perfect for storing my little treasures from the group at Odyssey. As I sit here now, I believe this has been the best week of my life, at least in terms of beginning to find out who I really am. I was not defined by motherhood or being a wife. I was just me. I am scared to go back to my life, but at the same time, I am beginning a whole new chapter of my life. I am excited about that.

March 26, 1998

I slept fitfully all night. Am ready to take a shower and get on with it. I have huge butterflies in my stomach. I even thought I was going to throw up. Thought of calling Harold, but he can't do a thing for me at this point. I have to go home. If I learned one thing last week it was: You can't judge people by what they do or what they look like. What truly counts is the spirit in people. I have wasted so much time withdrawing from people—either through fear or arrogance on my part. I shudder to think what I have missed out on. At least now I am getting a clue.

Left the El Conquistador in a rainstorm. Ended up sharing a cab to the airport with a therapist from New York who had been hired by Citibank to come out and talk to three hundred Citibank presidents about stress management and healthy business relationships. A real sweet, gentle man. I told him why I was there. He was compassionate and interested in everything I had to say. He refused to let me pay my share and said the kindest things to me when I left.

Talking to complete strangers on such a personal
level is so weird, because it seems to be happening
over and over to me. People seem to be reacting
differently to me now. I am bored stiff on the plane.
My seat was next to a nice guy, happily into his fourth
or fifth drink, so he was harmless. We talked about
travel, kids, and Myrtle Beach. When we landed he
offered me a ride home and I just smiled and said, "No
thanks, my husband is coming to pick me up."

Actually, I had to wake Ben out of a coma to come and pick me
up. It was a depressing homecoming. I wanted him to jump out of the
car and tell me how much he loved and missed me. Instead, he didn't
even get out of the car; he just sat there until I told him I had two bags,
so he drove over to the curb and parked. Great. The only man I want
love and attention from is a complete dope.

On the drive home, Ben asked, "You must be pretty tired
after Tucson."

"Yeah, I am."

"You sleep in. I'll get the kids off in the morning."

I went to bed and here is what I wrote before drifting off
to sleep.

...Home to Myrtle Beach. Deflated. I feel nothing but
emptiness and nothingness between us. We will never
survive....

Once home, during a session with Harold, I talked about
Tucson. It was tough to talk at first. I even cried a little as I went
through what had happened out there. "I think I'm taking the kids
over to the beach house today," I told him. I always feel so much better
over there.

I fell into a simple and easy rhythm as soon as I got to the
beach. I opened that screen door and the ocean winds pulled it out of
my grasp, slamming it into the side of the house. I usually wrapped
myself in a blanket and sat in one of the rocking chairs on the porch.

Sometimes, at sunset, I wrote in my journal or read a Melody Beattie book, trying to make sense of it all, trying to move on. One day, sweet little Olivia had found a dollar bill on the beach. Instead of spending it on herself, she went to a corner vending machine and returned with a Diet Coke and surprised me with it. She came up to me on the porch with a big smile on her face as I sat writing, wrapped her little arms around my neck, gave me a big kiss, and walked away.

Ben and I sat outside on the beach those first nights after I got back, talking about how much hard work our individual recoveries had been and will be in the future. We agreed there was still much to work on. As the sky darkened and we moved up to the porch, I felt more at peace than I had in a long time. Ben seemed to have felt the same way too.

Even so, I was torn between being home and being in Tucson.

March 28, 1998

It is high tide and really windy. Ben is meditating
before dinner. I need my privacy to write and work
on this journal. I have been telling Ben about Tucson.
I am feeling grateful for my family and grateful to
Ben for staying his course. I sometimes don't know
which way I am going. I feel vulnerable and raw. I
miss my new friends.

I always seemed to sleep better at the beach. After returning from Arizona, I found myself in a cycle of horrible dreams. Some of them were familiar but they had become increasingly more vivid. I would dream that Ben was in a room of women, and he was flirting and drinking. His eyes glassy, bloodshot, or half shut.

The second type of dreams were both disconcerting and comforting. In these dreams I was on my own, I had time to think about what I wanted to do, I was involved emotionally and physically with new men, men with no baggage and blue eyes. I'd awake from these dreams curious, not scared. It would only take Ben doing one stupid thing and I would remember that in my dreams he was just a twisted memory, a shadow I'd been drowning in, someone who had held my head underwater for too many years.

It turns out I came home to a mountain of bills and paperwork, and our checkbook balances were all screwed up. I was twenty states away recovering from what his backward world did to me, crying my eyes out for five straight days, and he couldn't pay the phone bill. Unbelievable.

April 2, 1998

It is a beautiful morning and I am so confused. I feel split in half; one side of me wants to stay married, the other half doesn't. Are things ever going to become clear? Here's my horoscope for the month: "Libra. Your astrological symbol is the scales. And if the stars are a true indication, right now your scales are up one moment then down the next, in seesaw fashion. There's an overload of planetary pushes and pulls influencing your horoscope, ensuring that this time of your life is a thrilling but testing and an uncertain phase. Recent, startling news that came from out of the blue also has seen you reconsidering your plans and expectations for the future. With passion running so high now, dramas are likely to continue to erupt." Boy, if that isn't exactly like my life right now.

With my dream life in full swing and the cast of dream men in it, I had lost all physical desire for Ben. He was a total turn off. When he touched me or held me, instead of finding comfort or disgust, I found myself thinking, *What would this feel like if it were someone else?*

My parents popped down for a visit around the same time the kids were out of school for spring break. Whenever they visited before, I looked at it as a relief from parenting for a while, but this trip, with my eyes newly adjusted from Tucson, I began to see things differently, including the way my father, a real curmudgeon sometimes, treated his granddaughters. When we were all together at church that Sunday,

my father wouldn't hold Olivia's hand. He said "it wasn't his style."
I couldn't believe it. Before I went to bed that night, I wrote about my
mother's relationship with the kids:

> The kids acted up with my parents at dinner. Because
> my father has a colostomy bag, he sometimes makes
> funny noises at the oddest times. Adults, of course,
> know what is going on when his body does that, but
> for kids, it is a different story. So, apparently during
> dinner when my father's stomach acted up, Harper
> said, "Grandpa, you farted!" Then, of course, all the
> kids started laughing. Unfortunately for Henry, he was
> sitting next to my mother. She slapped him hard on
> the back. The kids were appalled by that and couldn't
> wait to leave their condominium. I was angry that my
> mother hit Henry and upset at the same time that the
> kids were disrespectful to my father. When we got
> home, I sat them all down and lectured them about
> my father's illness and how he can't help making
> that noise. Then Harper felt badly, got upset, and I
> had her sit in my lap when the others went to bed.
> She was still scared seeing my mother hit Henry like
> that. I explained why my mother is the way she is –
> or at least I tried to. I don't know, sometimes I don't
> understand what makes her tick.

That incident made me reconsider moments in my own
childhood, like my mother's methods of making sure we had only
what we absolutely needed, and my father's way of filtering his love
for me through David. My parents' concern for their family's well
being was still one hundred percent, but the way they went about it
was just off sometimes.

We all went out to dinner at a place we love called Bovine's
in Murrells Inlet, two towns away. We discussed the goings-on of
everyone in the family. A major issue was the impending sale of our
parents' Wellesley house and the divvying up of the belongings. It was

our childhood home and held emotional ties. If this had been the only thing on my plate, it would have affected me far deeper than it did.

This brought up the subject of my younger brother, who should absolutely have been included in the drawing, despite my father's initial objections. Dad continued to maintain his position about my brother. They hadn't spoken so much as a few words to one another over the previous ten years. As soon as Dad became visibly uncomfortable discussing David, I looked him directly in the eye.

"From one parent to another, Dad," I said, "I cannot believe you want nothing to do with David, that you no longer love him, that you can turn off, like a light switch, the love you once had for him. I cannot accept that."

I knew it sunk in because Dad's eyes glazed over with tears, and after dinner he told me I was the only one who ever called him out on things like that. It was true. He rarely had to face the reality of his choices, and often it was because my mother deferred to my father when it came to major conflicts and decisions.

Ben, dull as a board all night, didn't jump in to give advice or join in our conversations. He just sat there and didn't say a word. The next day I wrote in my journal.

April 6, 1998

Woke up to a beautiful red sun rising over the ocean and streaming light into our bedroom. Unfortunately, Ben had eaten six servings of grilled garlic last night as an appetizer, and this morning every pore and orifice is oozing garlic. The kids and I are seriously grossed out. I got Harper and Olivia dressed and went to Wal-Mart to buy Easter supplies and spent a bloody fortune.

Hurried home and went for a glorious run. Not a cloud in the sky. I felt like a million bucks. The fear that has probably always been with me, that Ben will up and leave me for another woman, is gone. Right now, I feel beautiful, strong, and fairly certain that I could handle it, that I could actually survive reasonably well without him. When I look into the future, I don't see Ben in it. I see my kids and myself. I am beginning to take the attitude that I am grateful that Ben is here with me today—sexually sober and healthy. That is enough for me. The desire and dreams about other men coming into my life are still strong and I don't see anything wrong with that. I'm feeling liberated, both from Ben and from myself.

Having my parents around, after-all, is really nice. Having three generations walking down the beach together is so meaningful and beautiful. Then again, I'm a grown woman, and I see my parents differently. I see them as human beings with flaws and personalities, just like the rest of us.

April 8, 1998

I got out of bed at 9:00. I am so lazy. Felt depressed the minute I opened my eyes. My Al-Anon reading in the book, *Courage to Change,* was right on today. Deal with your past, acknowledge you may have harmed people, that you have been harmed, then move on, learn, and live your life for today. That put me in a better mood. I am writing on the back porch. It is cold, windy, and rainy at the beach. We are going to dinner with Bill and Laura tonight at the Gulf Stream Café. I can't wait to tell them about Tucson. They will be the first people I will tell everything to, besides Harold. I am feeling a little restless and sad at the moment.

"Have you discussed any of your work in Tucson with your parents?" Harold asked me at one of our sessions. I'd been discussing my feelings toward them, how difficult it still felt.

"That's not the kind of thing that they understand or want to listen to," I said. "They don't want to hear about therapy stuff."

"I think it might be a good idea for you to discuss it, perhaps in a letter. Do you think that is something you can work on?"

"I guess so," I said. Harold was pushing me harder than I liked, but not as hard as I could handle. He knew my breaking points by then, and that was one of the reasons I really appreciated him and his opinions. It seemed like just another bull-shit, emotional mountain to climb—to confront my parents after all this time had passed. I saw how they were with my brother, and I knew that unless I could get past their walls, I'd get crushed too. It's bad enough to be in your forties and discover your marriage is a fraud and your husband is a sex addict. But to throw in what could clinically be called an abusive childhood, all in the name of closure, I wasn't so sure what the point was. However, I agreed to it then and there in Harold's office, so now I had to do it.

Saturday

…Harold wants me to write a letter to my parents, letting them know how I feel about things in my childhood. God, I don't know where to begin. Why do I have to face all this shit at once?

Monday

…Finding out that my married life was a fraud was one thing; finding out my childhood was considered abusive is another. What it boils down to is, at the age of forty-one my real life starts. I have been living lie after lie all my life. This is shattering for me, as I have noticed that when I really think about everything that has been revealed to me this past year, I disappear into a fog. Harold wants me to start the letter but I just can't.

Thursday

…Harold is officially miffed that I didn't start the letter, so I promised him I would. I am going to write it over at the beach house.

Monday

…I have arranged the furniture around in the beach house, so I have a writing table and chair overlooking the porch, beach, and ocean. It is beautiful and peaceful, and there is nothing on the beach except the empty lifeguard stand. The letter to my parents just seems to flow easily.

Wednesday

I finished the letter. I have such mixed feelings about actually mailing this letter. I know it will be a great relief that they know how I feel about certain things and how some of their behaviors affected me. I don't know. Harold, while I'm in his office, makes it sound so right to mail it, but once I'm out of his office, I am filled with doubt. All this inner exploring is difficult and tiring. I can't bring myself to put it in the mail, yet.

My parents decided to do the drawing for all the furniture and stuff while my two older sisters were visiting. The five of us met in the kitchen of their rented oceanfront condominium.

My father had written a beautiful two-page letter for Henry explaining his Distinguished Flying Cross Medal, which I had framed. My nephews each received one too. My parents had written everything they no longer wanted on a legal pad, put all five names in the hat and pulled a name out for each item.

The funny thing was, almost every time my father reached in to pick a name, he seemed to draw David's. We all giggled at that, and even my Dad smiled after the fourth time in a row that David's name popped up. My father was still in so much emotional upheaval over his estrangement with my brother.

"That is likely something you could address after your parents read your letter," Harold had said, knowing of course, that I had not yet sent the letter.

"I am sure we will talk about it—that is, if they ever speak to me again after they read it," I responded.

May 10, 1998

…Something has snapped in me, for I have lost some
of the peace of mind and serenity I gained in Tucson.
I really have to focus every day on something that
has to do with recovery and find some time that I
can reconnect with all that I learned from Tucson.
I am impressed with Ben. To date he has remained
committed and is working his program. I am proud of
his daily courage and am so hopeful. Then, for some
reason, some thought enters my head that will throw
me into depression and resentment.

May 11, 1998

…My serenity and calmness have been broken
and I feel like I am almost back to my old self. I let
everything and everyone bring me down.

May 16, 1998

…Got into Boston late Tuesday night. David was there
to meet me. Stayed at his and Mike's place. Really neat
house. We stayed up till 2:30 talking. I shared some
stories about Ben and Mom and Dad and the girls
being down in Myrtle Beach. Went to bed exhausted
about 3 a.m.

Woke up early, sat around, and talked again. Told
David how hurt the kids are and started crying a little.
He did too. He seems happy with Mike and excited
about moving to New York. His relationship with Dad
is terrible, but David will not put up with any more
shit from him.

Took the train to Wellesley. Mom picked me up and
we went home. The house is pretty well packed up
and picked over. Went to lunch and did some errands
with Mom in downtown Wellesley. This town is still

beautiful. Went home, showered, and went to the
Club for dinner. David came and Lindsay joined us
later. The Country Club looks great—they re-did
it. Got up early and shipped my boxes and some
paintings that I picked from the drawing. Mom and
Dad drove me to the airport. They both got all dressed
up and looked really nice. I marveled a little at how
good they looked considering all the illness they
have been through. It was my father's fiftieth Boston
College reunion. He was voted Best Looking in his
class. "By default," he said.

Anyway, I drove off the hill for the last time. It was
a strange feeling, but at forty-one years of age, it is
about time to say good-bye to Abbott Road. Mom
and Dad dropped me off at the airport. We hugged
and I thanked them for everything. I felt pretty
relieved these days were over. I sat in the fucking
airport for five hours waiting to take off. Got gawked
at a couple of times. It is fun pretending I am single. I
was tired and annoyed by that point. Came home to a
comatose husband.

Harold really laid into me a couple of weeks in a row for not
wearing my wedding ring and being lax in his assignments for me. I
told him I'd only been going to one Al-Anon meeting a week, instead
of his recommended two or three.

I didn't feel married, so I wasn't wearing the ring. It was as
simple as that.

I didn't feel like sharing anything, so I wasn't going to the
meetings. Either I am too depressed to be there because I don't want
to cry, or I am too tired to drag my ass up there because I didn't
sleep well.

May 26, 1998

I chaired the Al-Anon meeting this morning. It was on
the subject of forgiveness—of which I haven't found
the secret. I am still so defensive and self-righteous.
I don't give a shit about Ben's feelings when I have
suffered so much at his hands. I think it would help
me if I found a sex addict group meeting. Is there
such a thing? It would be great to sit with a group of
women and hear their stories and share my fears with
them. I feel like a freak in Al-Anon.

Even with knowledge of my own laziness, I could feel myself
slipping out of the comfort zone that I can usually maintain when I
am regularly attending meetings. I woke up one morning after a long
night of horrible dreams and couldn't stop crying. I cried all morning
at Harold's, and then I cried in the afternoon and evening. I felt
isolated and didn't want to go home. I went to see the Sandra Bullock
movie, *Hope Floats*.

I could really identify with the entire movie. Her husband had
cheated on her, and the way she found out had blindsided her in a
similar way to what had happened to me. She had the strength to leave
him and start over again, something that I had wanted to do. Then she
ends up with a handsome new boyfriend, something I wished would
happen to me. My journal reflected my lingering hurt and confusion.

June 15, 1998

…I can't get beyond Ben's cheating, beyond his
betrayal. I just can't. I resent him nearly every time I
look at him, and it is painful right down to my bones.
I really love him, I know that in my heart. The crisis
before me is one of forgiveness and healing. I need
to allow myself to forgive him for his sick, sexual
betrayals. I want the intimacy in our marriage to
return. I'm sure of it.

During the next session with Harold, he looked at my left hand and said, "I notice you're still not wearing your wedding ring."

"I don't feel married to him," I explained. "Ben has been a horrible husband to me. I'm happy for him on a personal level because he is taking his recovery seriously, but I just don't feel married."

"I think for both your sakes, you should consider wearing it, and I'll leave it at that."

"OK, then."

June 21, 1998. Father's Day

I am poolside at 7 p.m. We just got home from the beach, and I am watching Henry eat a turkey sandwich. We had a good day today. Called my Dad to wish him a Happy Father's Day. Told him I prayed for him at church and there was dead silence. He is so uncomfortable with any show of emotion or intimacy. He is alone in Vermont—Mom is down at the Cape. I really wish I had a better relationship with him.

In the next journal entry, I wrote about God, because I had awakened at 6:15 in the morning to another beautiful sunrise.

June, 1998

For the first time in a long while I felt like I could hear God calling me to Him. I had an overwhelming need, an impulse, to go to church and just sit, to give thanks that we were healthy and all together. Ben, Olivia, and I went to church and reflected and prayed together. As soon as I knelt down, a woman, one of Ben's patients, came over to us. She was very sweet and introduced herself to me. She wanted me to know how much she liked having Ben as her doctor.

As she walked away, I resumed kneeling and began to whisper the "Our Father" prayer. I felt the words echo through my body, and I began to cry.

Eventually, we started going to the Myrtle Beach Community Church as a family, which was something new and positive for us. We slowly started going out together for dinners and movies, but only with new friends in recovery or people who were on a spiritual journey of some sort. The only old friends we continued to see regularly during that period were Laura and Bill and a handful of soccer parents.

We started to develop a close-knit group of recovery friends with whom we could be ourselves. I didn't feel like a fraud in front of them when Ben and I were together. These friendships were a nice surprise, because they were on a deeper emotional level than what I had typically experienced in previous relationships.

We continued to spend a lot of time at the beach, watching our children play with our dog, Roxie, who must have been the most obnoxious dog on the beach, running and kicking up sand. I watched the ocean with an understanding that I was witnessing something so much bigger than myself.

Ben, on the other hand, was staring at a young woman in a dress as she set up her chair and small blue umbrella on the beach a short distance from us. I knew what would follow and as she pulled her dress over her head to reveal a tiny bikini. I watched Ben's face. It became entirely clear that he couldn't pull his eyes away from her. In a moment of clarity, I reacted with patience, fighting back the urge to poke my finger in his eye. Yes, she was pretty, and, yes, she was younger than I was, but, so what? Beautiful women are everywhere. Gawking is disrespectful to me as his wife, to him as a recovering sex addict, and to that young girl, who is someone else's daughter.

"Maybe you should turn your chair the other way," I suggested.

"Maybe I should," he said. "You're right; I am distracted."

"You're not distracted—you are gawking."

This gawking business was such a touchy issue. It was so blatant and demeaning. I have a difficult time separating Ben's addict behavior from the Ben I love. Why the heck couldn't he just glance at an attractive woman and then move on? If he really wanted to, he could control himself.

Ben adjusted his chair, and when he snuck another peek, I stood up.

"I'm going for a run. I'll be back in a while."

Running on the beach has everything to do with simplicity. I can jump off the steps of my house, start running over the sand, and get my heart rate pumping. The movement of my body proves that I am made for action, not re-action. Running forces breathing, and almost nothing is better for a person who feels like she is being suffocated. You learn breathing as means for controlling rage, hysteria, sadness, or fear. A deep breath of cool, calming air will take the edge off of nearly anything sharp. Jogging on the beach at sunset will force anyone to breathe and breathe and breathe. I relished the exhilarating results of running, including how running could change my mood for the better.

Chapter Seven. Growing Pains

ℰℬ

Lightning storms often roll through Myrtle Beach with great intensity and little warning, at times in the middle of the night. I find the sounds of the wind and the rain calming as they move outside the beach house. One particular night when a major lightning storm hit, Ben was not at home.

The lightning lit up the sky and our beach house, the little rooms intermittently awash with light. The thunder that followed was so loud I thought Ella and Olivia would come running to my room and jump in bed with me. I almost hoped they would. The second bolt was bigger than the first, and the thunder rattled the house.

The girls slept right through it. I could understand Ella sleeping through it; she'd been so tired lately. After all, it was just a few nights earlier that I held her in my arms as she cried. Adolescence is agonizing enough, but knowing what she knows about her father and not being allowed to share that information made the transition even worse.

As a mother of a teenage daughter, I was happy to sit quietly and hold her as she wept. Her relationship with her father had become strained. Hugging was out of the question, I imagine, because of the guilt that Ben felt, and the awkward and confusing emotions that Ella was building toward men based on her once-heroic, now-flawed male role model.

I had mixed emotions as we sat on my bed, partly out of joy that I was part of the important moments in my daughter's life, and partly because I could not remember receiving this kind of love and empathy from my mother during my own years of teenage angst.

June 17, 1998

...Harold wants me to send my parents the letter. I still

have such mixed feelings about this. I fear it will really
hurt them, and I think they will be angry and think I
am ungrateful.

Summertime at the beach was easy for kids. They were free to
be more of who they really were. Herbie, our aging golden retriever,
tried to keep up but seemed to spend more and more time sleeping on
the porch, next to me and my journal.

Running the kids around to their various sports camps and
team practices had broken me out of my laziness for the moment. I had
once again started regularly attending Al-Anon meetings. I walked in
a few minutes late this particular morning and sat down in the closest
empty chair. A woman I didn't know well but recognized from the
kid's grammar school let out a audible gasp when she saw me.

She was emotional during the rest of the meeting and when
the meeting closed, she walked right over to me, crying, and gave
me the biggest hug. She told me that she was overwhelmed when
she saw me walk in the door, because she'd always been envious of
me, my husband, and my life with him. I was dumbfounded. I hadn't
considered that anyone could be jealous of my life.

I felt sad that she had been harboring resentment and envious
feelings toward me. So much wasted energy afforded to something
that had never really existed. I tried to comfort her as best I could,
and I gave her my number to call me if she wanted to talk or have
lunch someday.

Beth, a veteran of the program and the chairperson of that
particular meeting, watched my conversation with that woman. She
came up to me as I was leaving the building.

"You have this new aura about you," she said. "It's really
wonderful to see."

"Thank you, Beth, that means so much to me coming from
you," I said. Beth's comments really meant a lot to me.

July 1, 1998

I put my nice rings on again, but not my wedding ring.
I won't ever wear my wedding ring again. At least

this way my hands have enough jewelry on them to make it appear I'm married. Harold really got on my case again about it. I'm getting tired of the hassle. If I am going to cheat, I can do it regardless of that stupid ring. My stupid husband taught me that.

We went to mass, and we stayed the entire two hours. It was really beautiful. I am most moved by the music. I don't think Ben understands just how raw I feel. He is, at times, unsupportive and moody because of the kids and my no-sex rules. He's wrapped up in himself.

July 3, 1998

…Had a rough time with Harold yesterday. He told me he was glad I put the rings back on but after our session Tuesday, he was really concerned about me. He called a therapist friend of his to discuss my situation because H. feels he isn't getting through to me—that I am stuck. Great.

July 11, 1998

Ben and I have the house to ourselves—all the kids are gone for the night. He has been very miserable lately and has been thinking about relapse. It is so hard for me to understand that he loves me and he loves his children, but at times he thinks about just picking up and leaving all of us and acting out again. How bizarre to think that a man can give everything up for a moment in time! Read about eighty pages of *The Road Less Traveled*. I am determined to read an hour a day of something that will help my condition—whatever that is.

July 13, 1998

Yesterday was weird. Spent a glorious day on the
beach. Felt increasingly rejected by Ben as the day
wore on. He didn't speak much and looked annoyed if
I talked to him about what I was reading. When I told
him his behavior today was remote and closing me
out, he arrogantly asked me to rephrase my feelings.
I said, "I feel rejected," and he just looked at me and
didn't acknowledge anything I said. I got angry and
went inside the house. Later we talked about it, and I
acknowledged where I was wrong. Ben had a harder
time admitting his arrogance and condescending
behavior. He said, "When you phrase your feelings
appropriately, then I will respond to you." Who the
fuck does he think he is?

I am doing OK but feel very scattered. I can't focus on
one task and see it through. I have lost the ability to
think as an adult. My fucking car got keyed! I wonder
if that is covered by insurance?

I spent the next few days quietly wasting my time on the beach
in my bikini top and my cut-off jean shorts, just reading mindless
magazines and listening to music. A guy around my age commented on
my hair. He had been staring at me the entire time I was there. It was
uncomfortable, so I got up to leave, which is when he approached me.

"Oh, you aren't leaving are you? You're the sole reason for
my existence."

I just smiled at him and left.

I should have felt disgusted, because it was such a lame
comment, and it was the same behavior I would happily harpooned
Ben for doing. But, I can't lie, it did feel nice. Along with the pain and
constant changes that Ben's disclosure has brought us, there were still
the self-inadequacy issues that told me I was not good enough in bed
or attractive enough. It doesn't matter how many times a woman hears
that she had nothing to do with her husband's sex addiction, I still felt

that way. I felt ugly and undesirable, and if it took some guy on the beach, with a beer and cooler, to unabashedly hit on me to remind me that I still had what it takes, then so be it.

"That's a double standard to deal with," Harold said when I told him about the guy on the beach.

"I don't intend on actually doing anything with anyone, so, no, it is not a double standard."

"You know what I mean. You can't spend the morning making sure Ben is not staring at women on the beach, then spend the afternoon being a woman who is stared at," he said.

Oh, brother. Harold is exhausting.

July 17, 1998

…I lost it with Ben last night. He went to an AA meeting from 8 to 9, but he came home a little after 10:30—with no phone call. I flipped out. I really was positive he relapsed. I even made him call his friend, who he claimed to be with, to confirm where he was. Turns out, he was telling the truth. He really did help him change a flat tire. I can't trust anything he has to say. My spirit is so broken.

July 22, 1998

…We had a horrible night out. Full of anticipation— all dressed up and no place to go. Went to the Bistro Restaurant. Ben was cold, distant, unloving. Nothing seems right. For the hundredth time I am in my car riding home after a night out with my husband and have an overwhelming feeling of sadness and loneliness and want to jump out of the car.

July 25, 1998. Olivia's Birthday!

…Today was a happy day—my little Olivia turned eight. We had a fun birthday party for her. I have just completed the final draft of the letter. I have to make

a copy for myself and one for Harold's files. I am
actually sick of writing it, so I am relieved it is finally
done and ready to mail.

August 1998

...I'd been watching the coverage of President Clinton
and Monica Lewinsky, and I cannot believe today's
events. The Congress made public the Starr Report,
and it is incredible—very graphic details about the
president and his sexual encounters. Our president is
a sex addict, and now the entire world knows about
sexual addiction. I am glued to the coverage as they
talk about impeachments proceedings. I am angry and
intrigued at the same time to know I am not alone in
my hurt and betrayal and humiliation. I cannot believe
how Hillary can bear having it all made public. If
Ben's addiction had been made public, I would have
died from shame and embarrassment. I guess that's
why I am not where she is sitting, and why I am sitting
here. I feel like I should e-mail her. I am totally out of
sorts. This stress is making me physically ill. I think I
either have AIDS or cancer.

I realized later that coverage of the Clinton scandal was
constantly triggering pain and anger for me. I was at the beach house
when President Clinton made his announcement that, yes, he lied,
and he did have sex with Monica Lewinski. I had tears in my eyes as I
watched his speech to the American people. I kept thinking about Hilary
and her daughter in the White House, knowing that their private agony
and humiliation was going to play out on a public stage. Our daughter,
Ella, was very upset too. She asked if her Dad had had sex with younger
women like that. The Clinton scandal had a big impact on my family
and me—and no doubt on millions of others. As I was processing my
emotions and coming to grips with the truth of my marriage, I was
watching the ruin of the Clintons' very public marriage.

My private struggle with Ben's infidelity had morphed on to the front pages of every newspaper and news magazine in the world. As I walked through Barnes and Noble, all I saw were images of Monica Lewinsky wearing that nutty beret, standing in some receiving line, smiling and looking up adoringly as the President shakes people's hands and passes by her. The President should be the figurehead for all that is good with America, politics, and morality in this country, not the opposite. What a joke.

I watched the coverage of the Clinton family boarding a plane. It was the first time I had seen Hilary on TV since the President's admission. The look on her face was a clear mixture of pain and incredible anger at her stupid husband's behavior. It was stunning. I could actually feel it. I was where she was. She was handling it with such profound dignity and courage. If I ever get stuck in a foxhole, I want her in there with me. Watching their daughter walking in the middle, between her parents, holding their hands was a poignant image.

At one of our Al-Anon meetings, we were absent a chairperson, and one of the regulars asked me to do it. I had no problem chairing meetings and the comfort I felt doing it was a constant reminder of how far I'd come from cowering in the doorways and trying to sit alone.

I started talking about the Clinton issues and how they were getting to me. Because there were at least four other women there who I knew to be safe and trustworthy, I launched into my own personal struggles with my husband's infidelities. I didn't discuss the great lengths he had gone to, but I did apparently hit on an interesting and sensitive nerve among the group, because everyone began sharing their own experiences.

One woman said she learned her husband had had one affair and it tore her apart. To that day, she hadn't gotten over his affair, and because of it, their relationship was changed forever. She went on to say that, later, getting over his death to cancer had been easier than getting over his single affair that had happened more than twenty years earlier. An overwhelming number of other people said they, too, have had fantasies about leaving their addicted husband's behind and starting a new life with a new man.

It was nice to leave the meeting and stop judging myself for my thoughts and fantasies of other men. It is, apparently, a natural thing to do in the wake of being the victim of infidelity.

One day Harold asked me, "Have you found yourself a serious sponsor in Al-Anon yet?"

"Not really," I said. "I have connected with one woman a little —I have been over to her house a couple of times. I don't see the point of having an Al-Anon sponsor. I need a woman who is married to a sex addict to be my sponsor."

"Well, I think you are getting stuck again."

"I don't think so. I wrote the letter to my parents. Isn't that what you wanted me to do?"

"Yes, you did. I'm just not sure how it will help your relationship with either your mother or your father if it sits on your desk at home next to your wedding ring." He, of course, noticed I wasn't wearing a ring again. Harold looked back at me, waiting to see what excuse I would come up with.

"But I haven't found a healthy ground between detaching from Ben and being close and loving toward him," I told him. "How do you expect me to wear a ring that says my marriage was a complete lie? Wearing a wedding ring means nothing to me anymore."

"How would you feel if Ben stopped wearing his ring?" Harold asked.

"I don't think I'd care," I answered. "If it never mattered to him when he was bellied up to a stripper pole, then what the hell does it mean now?"

"Mo," Harold said. "I believe you are getting seriously stuck in your healing, and I want you to do something different, something a little more intense.

I remember seeing the words I'd just written in my journal a day or two before: "I feel down most of the time, and, coupled with my overall do-nothing-but-the-bare-minimum-road-of-recovery, I don't know how much longer I can take all of this."

It was around the time, when I was being pressured to seek more in-depth treatment, that I wrote the following in my journal about loneliness.

I am so sick and tired of feeling such a sense of
loneliness. Kids and people surround me all day long,
yet I have this incredible emptiness that cannot be
filled. I have been telling Harold that I need to get
a dog, just for me, and he has jumped all over me
about that. But I couldn't take it anymore, so I went
to the Horry County Animal Shelter after one of my
sessions with Harold. After walking up and down
two rows of dogs who were barking in their cages, I
found the one I was supposed to adopt. This beautiful,
thin, golden retriever just sat there by the kennel
door, leaning against it, not barking at all. She had
beautiful greenish-brown eyes and looked so sad. I
kept coming back to her cage and looking at her and
finally I realized why. I was looking at her because she
reminded me of me. Sad with green eyes. I adopted
her on the spot. I had to drop her off at the local vet for
a physical. It turns out she has to be treated for heart
worm and has been terribly over-bred. She is maybe
three years old but has the stomach of a much older
dog. She is the perfect dog for me.

After I brought the dog home, I wrote the following
journal entry.

...Here I sit out at the pool with my new dog, Tucson.
I have decided to name her that because my life really
began in Tucson during the first therapy week, and
now this dog is starting a happy new life with us.
Harold is going to kill me; I can hear him now—"A
dog cannot fill your emptiness." Oh, yes she can. She
will love me unconditionally. She is so sweet, doesn't
take her eyes off me. She hasn't made a peep yet.

Harold wanted me to go the Meadows Treatment Center in
Arizona. He had an informational package overnighted to me from

the Meadows. I opened it, and Good God, its price was worse than Menninger for a five-week program. I said, Forget it. I decided to call Harold and tell him I will agree to go away again but not to that crazy place.

I talked to Harold on the phone. He laughed when I asked about the detox thing and how freaky it seemed. He said they would tailor my treatment program for my needs. "Well, if I don't have to detox from anything, then why in the world do I have to go away for so long?" He told me to calm down and call the place in the morning and see what I thought.

I called Arizona the next morning and decided that place was not for me. Harold is not happy I declined the Meadows. I agreed to go somewhere, so now there is some dopey place in Tennessee I have to look at.

On-Site is located in Nashville, Tennessee. After looking at the brochures, I agreed to go. Ben was all for it, so there wasn't a problem there.

The same day, Ben suggested we go out.

"I think we should have an evening out. We'll get a bite to eat and talk some things over," he said.

We went to the brand new Friendly's restaurant, and much to my satisfaction, their chocolate Fribble (New England speak for "shake") tasted just like the ones I'd enjoyed while growing up in Wellesley.

"I have to ask you something," I said to Ben.

"OK," he answered slowly.

"How much is it bothering you that I'm not wearing my wedding ring? It really bothers Harold. He thinks I am doing it to make you feel badly."

"I don't like that fact that you don't wear one, so, yes, it does bother me." He said.

"But you understand why I don't want to wear it?" I asked.

"Yeah, and I know there is nothing I can do to change that."

I saw during those moments, a real hurt coming from Ben, his face, his eyes and body language.

We left Friendly's and went to a small jewelry store and bought a simple gold band. It would be my new wedding ring, and it represented a fresh start. We went to the House of Blues to celebrate, and while we sat at the bar, Ben looked in my eyes and didn't falter. He told me how sorry he was, apologizing for it all, saying some truly beautiful things, and asking for my forgiveness.

"I never want to go back to that lifestyle, ever," he said. "I want to spend the rest of my life being the best husband and father that I can be."

"I'd be a liar if I told you that I forgive you at this very moment," I responded, "but I do really want to someday be able to put all this behind me and really forgive you from my heart. I am just not ready."

"I hope so," he said. "Letting you know how truly sorry I am for what I have done is so hard for me to do. I don't want to realize and comprehend the damage I've done; I think if I had to come to terms with that, I would probably kill myself."

"I don't know what to say, Ben. It is hard for me to put myself in your shoes."

I have been waiting for this day to come for a long, long time. Ben knew what he had done and he was sorry for the damage, but he could not fully face it yet. He was not strong enough yet. This discussion started with one simple question about me not wearing a wedding ring. We were finally finding hope when we least expected it.

Chapter Eight. A Spiritual Awakening

§)(R

As I have said before, I sleep better at the beach house. It must be the subtle rhythm of the ocean lulling my eyes closed. As long as Ben's snoring doesn't keep me awake, I can sleep a full six or seven hours, uninterrupted.

I had been having vivid dreams, mostly about Ben and sexual addiction stuff, and me being victimized or attacked. One night, I had an intense dream about Ben relapsing and my guardian angel—or spiritual guide, whatever you want to call it. This guide was taking me through scenes in my life to show me how angels are always present and looking after us. Some had wings with just a faint outline, and they dressed in dark, plain clothing.

My guardian angel showed me a car full of wild teenagers driving out of control. Their angels were sitting up on the back of the car as their convertible swerved in and out of traffic. They arrived safely to their destination despite the horrible odds that they could have crashed the car.

The last scenario was of Ben. My guide and I visited him during his addict days, surrounded by a group of sleazy women. Ben's eyes were glassy, and I could see his wedding ring from the faint light of the jukebox located near his bar stool. Three guardian angels surrounded him, but Ben seemed unaware of them.

That vivid dream made me see that no matter what anyone does, we are all God's children and we are under his protection of angels who keep us safe. Regardless of what Ben did, he was forgiven and loved. As I woke up from the dream, it still felt real, like I had actually learned a huge lesson.

So life goes on. About two months after I had this dream, Ben and I decided to do something fun and see a Hall and Oates concert at the House of Blues.

August 20, 1998

...I am excited to go to the concert because I haven't
been out to a normal, fun place since this nightmare
started. Also made reservations at the hotel at
Broadway at the Beach, so we don't have to drive
all the way home. Harold said fine about the concert
as long as I go to the open AA meeting with Ben
first. He is concerned about Ben being in a concert
environment—too much stimulation. If that is what
it takes I will do it. Got dressed for the concert—have
lost some weight and am wearing my skinny jeans.
Ben looked great in jeans, loafers, and shirt.

First stop was an AA meeting, open to AA members, their
family, and anyone who might be interested in the program. The
subject of the meeting was relapse or slip-ups. Some of the sharing was
self-serving, some was flat out boring, some was funny, and some was
sad. It was a good mix; it was the first open AA meeting that I actually
enjoyed and felt better for going.

Got to the House of Blues and the concert was great. Had a
wonderful time. Did not get caught up in monitoring Ben and whether
or not he was looking at girls. I loved the music and could have cared
less what he was doing.

After we checked in to the hotel, we watched a movie called
City of Angels. Within a few minutes into the movie, I freaked. The
angels in this movie were exactly the same as the angels in my dream
from a couple of weeks ago! Same clothing, same expressions on
their faces, same affect. I was positively overcome. I started weeping
uncontrollably, and then experienced the most intense feeling of love
that I have ever felt. With my eyes still closed from weeping, I had
the vision of a figure in white surrounded by a bright light. It was
the most powerful emotional experience I have ever had. Slowly, the
vision and the intense feeling subsided, and I was able to tell Ben what
had just happened. He was wonderful. He held me as I described the
experience, and he never doubted or questioned what had happened.

My favorite part of the movie was the beginning when the little girl dies; once she sees her angel, she calms down and is unafraid to die as her spirit departs from her body and takes the hand of her guardian angel. Angels really do exist.

Also in the movie, the angels gather at the beach in the evening to watch the sun slip behind the clouds and sink into the ocean. They hear a beautiful orchestra and choirs of angels in heaven. I now believe in angels and the healing power of the ocean and what it represents.

Later I shared this experience with Harold. He nodded his approval as I told him about what had happened as I watched that movie and made the connection to my dream. Talk about a spiritual awakening.

"How are you feeling about heading down to Tennessee this week?" he asked, referring to the week-long, intensive therapeutic workshop.

"I'm ready to go. I think Ben can't wait to get rid of me. I'm not too excited about bearing my soul in front of a group of new people, but I didn't want to do it the last time either."

"I think you'll find that you'll be able to pick up where you left off," Harold said. "That's what I'm hoping for you. You definitely need a change of pace."

"I hope you are right, Harold." I said.

He was happy to see the new, simple wedding ring from my night out with Ben. He was pleased that I had taken his advice and had found a common ground on my own instead of fighting Ben about wearing the old ring.

Just as he finished that sentence, my heart jumped in my throat. My new gold band slipped off my finger and when I went to grab it, it slipped right through a tiny hole in the upholstery, underneath the cushion and into the belly of Harold's green leather couch. Sheepishly, I had to interrupt our session and tell Harold what had just happened. I jumped off the couch, we flipped it over and unfortunately, Harold had to slit the couch open with a scissors, stick his hand in and fish around for the ring. A few minutes went by before he found it. The entire time, Harold muttered under his breath. He stood up and handed me the ring.

"I think we're done for today," he said with irritation in his voice. "I'll see you in a week when you get back."

I left the office thinking, Uh oh, I think Harold is sick of me. Come to think of it, I'm sick of me.

Not long after, I decided to take Harold's advice; I mailed the letter to my parents. A few days later I wrote in my journal.

> …I am very anxious and upset about my parent's reaction to the letter. They got it either Saturday or today. I read the book *Back from Betrayal*, by Jennifer Schneider. It is my new favorite book. The first half dealt with facts and reasons why I married someone like Ben. It is very painful stuff—realizing how sick and needy and low I allowed myself to become. In the book, the author even used some of my answers from a survey I filled out for her. Ben's doctor from Menninger, Dr. Irons, sent me the questionnaire.

> My letter to my parents has been mailed. Now I had to wait for a response.

> Below is the letter I wrote my parents.

July 22, 1998

Dear Mom and Dad,

This is a letter written out of love and in partnership with my recovery process and is not meant to be perceived at your expense.

Because of what happened to my marriage in July of last year, I have been thrown into the world of therapy, self-examination and recovery from emotional trauma. I have been reviewing my life, beginning with my childhood memories—all to understand how and why I got to the point of last July.

I am going through this process with the help of weekly sessions with a therapist and a couple

meetings a week with a local Al-Anon group. I
went through an intense, life-altering self-discovery
workshop out in Tucson. Neither of you asked me
any real questions about that week. I don't know if it
is because you are afraid to get too close to me or you
don't care to know, or what—but you are my parents,
after all. Why don't you want to know me on a more
intimate level?

I view the workshop out in Tucson as a real
turning point in my life. I was given the opportunity
to explore my childhood and adolescence, growing up
in the big house on Abbott Road.

I will start with you, Dad. I realized that I
had and still have such an enormous amount of love
and respect for you—admiration for your integrity,
your off-beat sense of humor, unwavering sense of
what is honorable and fair. You worked day after day
to provide for your family and really succeeded at it.
You did it on your own with no financial help from
anyone. I am unquestionably proud of what you have
accomplished and admire you for how well you have
taken care of us financially.

I believe the sadness and tears come because,
on an emotional level, when I think of you I feel such
a sense of loss and a big hole in my life. As your
third child and daughter growing up in our family,
I missed out on a lot from you—in that important
father/daughter relationship. I can never remember
you holding me or comforting me and talking about
anything meaningful, except for one or two instances.
To my recollection you never hugged me and you
have never told me that you love me, ever.

As a matter of fact, the only nice thing you
ever said to me that I can remember was that I was
well coordinated! I felt totally inferior being a girl;
you seemed to have used most of your free time and

energy concerned with doing things with David. I felt
invisible and didn't matter that much to you. There is
a home movie of us at the Cape where we are playing
baseball on the beach. I was probably five, David
was three. You were pitching and I was the catcher,
and David was at bat. You let David swing and miss
forever, and I can remember hoping and wishing you
would want to see me at bat, but once David didn't
want to play anymore, you both just stopped playing
and walked away. The message I got from you that
day, and many other times throughout my childhood,
was that I didn't matter as much to you because I was
a girl. It seemed that almost every time you were given
Red Sox or Celtics tickets, you always wanted to take
David when I would have loved to be included too.

I feel a sense of loss from your lack of reaching
out to me in another way as well. I felt you never
expected anything out of me, never sat me down and
had the hard talks about my life, goals, what I wanted
to be. Although you were always patient when I asked
for help with my homework, you never came to me;
I always came to you. I went through my school and
early college years believing I wasn't very bright and
would never amount to much on my own. It wasn't
until years later, when I graduated from Coastal with
my political science degree that I was able to realize
that I am actually quite smart and my teachers enjoyed
having me in their classes.

Dad, you are such a paradox to me because
some of the things I admire about you are also the
very things I have problems with you as an adult. An
example is your Catholic faith and you standing up for
something you believe in. The Church, above all else,
teaches us not to judge—only God can do that—and
that forgiveness is essential to spiritual growth. Your
behavior toward your son is the most glaring example

of how two such principles that I know you believe in, have run amok. Your devastating lack of tolerance and suspension of emotional love and understanding have torn this family apart. And we have all suffered in different ways. I know you are suffering, both physically and emotionally. Mother has suffered because your behavior and inability to cope with having a gay son have forced her to choose between keeping the peace at home with her husband versus having a loving relationship with her own son. I know you love Mother, so I can't understand why you would place such a heavy burden on her shoulders.

David has suffered beyond measure. The things you have said to him and your rejection of him as a member of our family have been horrific and devastating to him, I am sure. He told me some of things you said to him that awful day he came out and I can't believe that a father would ever say that to his own son, let alone my father saying it to my brother. It is painful for me, as a forty-one year old, to watch someone who is so important to me live his life so closed off from the people who love him the most. We all lose.

With you, Mom, I have more anger and resentment and questions. There are many things that I admire and respect about you as well. Your artistic talents for one—you are a gifted artist. I love your energy and spontaneity, your constant quest to travel and explore someplace different and learn new things, and your ability to make friends easily and how you seem to be willing to try anything (within reason) once.

However, what I took for normal discipline may not have been that at all. The slapping, pulling of hair, washing my mouth out with soap, and all the constant yelling at me was really out of control, and, in some circles, considered abusive behavior. That has been devastating for me to come to terms with. This great family in this great, beautiful house up on the hill was for a lot of years a very dysfunctional, chaotic household. A lot of this, from my perspective, was brought about by your rage at me and the other kids.

As an adult, I can understand where some of that rage came from. Having your father die at an early age—and having to deal with that awful loss—as well as an incredibly unhappy, demanding mother, was a lot to deal with. Going through miscarriages, raising five kids pretty much on your own, as Dad never seemed to really help out with the day-to-day operations, really must have pissed you off. So I can understand your anger; I have it as well. We, your children, took the brunt of your rage. You scared me as a child, and you even scared some of my friends. I never remember feeling loved or nurtured by you. You certainly cared for me well, made a beautiful home for us to grow up in. I never remember you hugging me, holding me, kissing me, or listening calmly to me. I think that every time you turned your back on me emotionally, or slapped me, especially across the face, squashed my spirit as a little girl, your daughter.

Two distinct memories come to mind that I do want to share with you. It was the day of Kennedy's funeral procession on TV. You both had us all kneel down in the library as we watched the black-and-white TV. We all knew you were both upset at what we were watching, but I didn't really understand the whole thing. At any rate, I started giggling at something, and one of you—I think it was Dad—slapped me really hard across the face. I fell off my knees, stunned, humiliated, and hurt that you would lash out at me like that, out of nowhere. To this day, I have never slapped any of my kids across the face or pulled their hair and could never imagine doing that. Olivia is turning eight in two days and I just wince even thinking about that happening to her. It is such a horrible, humiliating thing to do to a child.

I do remember how concerned you were when I broke my nose, and I remember how special I felt when you told me you would buy me anything I wanted (a Give-A-Show projector). That was a great moment in my life. The sad part is I had to break a bone to feel loved and wanted by either of you.

In closing, I want you to know I am sincerely grateful how you both came through for me in my time of need. I will never forget what you both did. Mother, it was the first time I remember that you said you loved me. And you both hugged me, not because we were saying good-bye, but because you both were willing to share in my pain. I will never forget that week and everything you did for me, and I think it was a real turning point in my relationship with the both of you.

I deeply regret that my problems with Ben and the events of this past year have caused you any worry and heartache. My wish for you both after reading this is to understand that this is not meant to blame either one of you for the adult choices I have made in my life. I hold myself one hundred percent responsible for what has happened and where I find myself today.

I am told by my therapist that writing a letter like this allows me to unburden things that I have carried around with me and impact how I react to things as an adult. At forty-one, I would say I am more than ready to let go of my childhood and adolescent emotional baggage. For me to do that, I feel I have to let you both know what thoughts and memories are

inside me. I know it will help me just because I will
have the knowledge that you have read the things that
have been imbedded in my brain and in my heart.

Love,
Your daughter,

   Maurita

I worried so much, for so long, that this letter would upset
my parents. But it didn't. All that worrying for nothing. Harold was
right; it had been important to get it off my chest and, at the same time,
be totally honest with my parents. Their only comment was from my
Mom. "You were right on about what you said about your Dad and
your brother." It turned out they understood the reasoning behind
sending such a letter.

September 29, 1998

…Finished filling out this long, boring, nosey
questionnaire from On-Site. I can't wait to get this over
with. Then, when I get back from Nashville, we leave
for Asheville and Maggie Valley for one of Harold's
mountain therapeutic spiritual goofiness.

I had no expectations of what was going to come out of my
week at Onsite. I'd gotten past Harold being annoyed with me for
attending Onsite instead of the Meadows like he had wanted. "I'm
not that sick," I told him. "I'm just confused and scared and tired all
the time. I don't think going to a nutty, hard-core rehab center for five
weeks is necessary."

I wanted to solve for myself three things, and I made a list
during my trip out there:

1.   I want to find the answer to the questions, "Am I staying
     in my marriage out of fear of rejection, being alone, being
     financially responsible for myself for the first time in a
     long time? Being financially responsible for my children?
     Or am I staying because I really do love him and it is the
     right thing to do?"

2. Clarify what behaviors of mine are destructive, holding me back, or unhealthy for my spiritual recovery.
3. I want to know how to get my spirit back, to feel human and whole again.

I had the same awkward feelings that a person gets when meeting strangers who will soon reveal their deepest feelings, just like my experience in Tucson. This time, it was a bit easier as I knew what to expect. Still, it was awkward; there are no two ways about it.

This time, the group was four men and three women, and a bear of a man named Jake was our therapist. And here's a sentence I never thought I'd be writing with such enthusiasm: "I finally met some sex addict men who are into pornography, prostitutes, and strip clubs. At last!"

They were married men who were agonizing about coming to terms with their behaviors and the chaos and destruction they were dealing with on the home front. I thought it ironic, that instead of looking at them with disgust and anger, I actually felt compassion for them. It blew me away how willing they were to be vulnerable and wounded enough to show real emotion and real remorse. I wish I could see more remorse and emotion from Ben.

My husband had not been able to share emotions and vulnerability on the level that these men were able to. I was beginning to understand that combining our individual recoveries, our unstable marriage, and parenting responsibilities was terribly challenging.

I experienced moments in clarity that I wished I could bottle up and access in times of pain and confusion.

One of the members in our group, a pretty, thin, and athletic woman a few years younger than me, had the most profound effect on me. Her name was Celia, and I am increasingly certain that she was the reason I was sent to Nashville. God wanted me to meet Celia.

Celia's father was a big-time sex addict and had been throughout her life. He was not in recovery, as he believed he was doing no harm. Celia's office was downtown, and several times a week she'd see her father's truck parked at one of the seedy bars on the main street. She and I are both from large families. She had two sisters and one brother, much like our Henry and the girls.

Everything she said during that week made such an impact on me. Meeting and listening to Celia was a window into the future of my daughters, a future that would exist if their father didn't stay the course of his recovery and their mother buried her head in the sand. Celia's mother had thought her husband's problems were long over when he admitted to having several affairs during Celia's childhood.

But her mother didn't know what Celia knew. She didn't know about the bar routines and the late nights. And because Celia's mother was already practically a shell of a woman, the kids didn't talk about it with her. They didn't confront their father about it either, and it practically ate her family alive.

I cried so hard listening to her talk about her adoration for her father as a young girl and how his infidelities and behaviors impacted some of the struggles she'd had with her own relationship and men in general.

It is all a cycle, and the only way to break the cycle or change it for good is through hard work, the kind of work you don't want to do even after you've thought you have finished—harder than journaling, harder than giving your testimony at a meeting.

It would have been so easy just to hate Ben with my entire being and stay in the marriage raising the kids with one eye open to their needs and one eye closed to my own. That would have been easier than confronting the demons head-on. The din of Ben's childhood still echoed in his life, just as my childhood still brought discord to my life. Now, Ben and I were making noise in our own children's lives, and we needed to fix it for them, if not for ourselves.

"I'm ruining my children by staying married, aren't I?" I asked Celia through sobs.

"No, you aren't, Maurita. There is still time. In fact, there is a lot of time. You and your husband are willing to do the work."

I have a feeling that we will be connected with each other for the rest of our lives. I hope she finds a way to love herself, to find peace of mind and a loving relationship with someone who is kind and treats her with the love that she deserves. When Celia left On-Site, she left me a note that I glued into a page in my journal.

Maurita,

Your strength and determination amaze me. I admire
your willingness to continue on your path as a mother.
Your life has not been a fraud. Much peace will come
to you, in time, as a result.

—Celia

The greatest gift I received from my week at On-Site was
meeting so many other people who had been impacted, in different
ways, by sex addiction. I no longer felt like such a loser, a freak.

That first weekend back from Tennessee, we were having
a family day at the beach. Ben, Henry, and the girls ran around the
beach, a picture-postcard of a happy family. All of a sudden there was
panic on the beach. An older man ran up the beach from the water's
edge and yelled out to a lifeguard that someone had gone under.

The lifeguard radioed it in and all the lifeguards from the
other stations up and down the beach ran toward the spot where the
man had gone under. Ben ran down to the water's edge with the other
lifeguards. His years of experience and instincts as a lifeguard on the
Jersey Shore kicked in. The lifeguards and Ben immediately began
searching in a human chain, moving side by side into the water and at
times, diving under the surface, looking for the man.

Volunteers joined the search, and Harper, Ella and Henry, all
reasonably strong swimmers, joined their Dad, diving and surfacing,
and diving again. I stayed on our beach house steps with Olivia, who
was scared and had curled into my arms. They'd been searching for
fifteen minutes when we heard the lifeguard's whistle signaling that
the man had been found. By then, the emergency vehicles had arrived
and they pulled the man out of the water and carried him to the back
of the ambulance. The section of water they pulled him from was
where all of us had gone into the water to swim a million times before.

The beach was so silent. It seemed as if even the crash of the
waves had gone silent out of respect, as I sat holding Olivia, who had
begun to shake.

I was reminded of the precarious nature of life. I had spent so much time feeling sorry for myself and resenting Ben's selfish and sick decisions, that I had forgotten to count my blessings.

Seeing Ben sprint into that water after the lifeguards, willing to risk everything to save someone else, reminded me of what kind of man he really is. I remembered that he would lose everything to save me if I encountered peril like that. Sometimes he buried those redeemable qualities beneath several layers of bullshit, but so does everyone else.

Seeing him charge the water like that, seeing our kids charge right in after him, without questioning it, eager and ready to help, reminded me that Ben still has that core of goodness and undeniable selflessness that, against all odds, had been passed on to our children. As they stood there watching the team work on the man they'd tried to save together, Ben's hands were on his hips and he was breathing hard.

I covered Olivia's ears as the emergency truck drove directly past our beach house steps; the paramedics were doing chest compressions on the young man, his legs hanging limp off the back of the truck as they passedby.

Sadly, the young man did not survive. He was already gone before they pulled him from the water. He left the world suddenly, too early perhaps. In this tragedy, my entire family learned of our strength as a unit and as a team. We learned that there are sometimes days and weeks of anger and pain, but we are there for one another, and we are there for good. We learned that we don't always have as much time together as we'd like to have, and that each day should be treated as a gift. We learned that any life is worth saving, and sometimes it takes a team of people preserve that life. At times, we might fail, but we must try, nonetheless. As a family, we have to keep trying too.

Chapter Nine. Who's Your Gail?

෫ාශ

When I received a card from my father for my birthday, I smiled. This was the first written communication I had received from either of my parents since sending them the letter, and I was thrilled to get my usual birthday card and note from my father.

Inside my father's card was a check for $42 with a yellow post it note attached: "Happy Birthday—COURAGE!"

What a perfect word and sentiment for him to write. I certainly needed a lot of courage. We regularly do readings from *The Book of Courage* in Al-Anon, so when you feel you need that brand of Al-Anon courage, this book is perfect for that. The Serenity Prayer is also right on the mark and deals with courage too:

God, grant me the serenity
To accept the things I cannot change,
The courage to chance the things I can,
And the wisdom to know the difference.

I spent so much of my day being scared of one thing or another. I feared Ben would relapse, I feared I would lash out in anger and alienate Ben and the kids. I feared that we would go into debt from all the therapy, and, ironically, going into debt would make me need more therapy!

One of the valuable lessons I learned as part of my week in Tennessee was being able to examine the way I "hid" or "checked out" from the daily stresses of my life. I realized I need to be aware of why I do certain activities. For example, why can't I enjoy a couple of glasses of wine at night after the kids are washed and tucked in? I can. Why can't I go shopping whenever I want as long as I'm not overspending? I can. Why can't I watch three or four hours of television a day? Why can't I just listen to music alone in my room while Ben and the kids are home?

I can. But I have learned that doing all of those things every day, or even more than one at a time, is escapism. And escaping my family isn't helpful to me or to them. If you add in my furniture painting, work-out schedule, Al-Anon meetings, and solo therapy with Harold, there was not enough time in the day.

Harold had told me before I went to On-site that mixing wine with anger issues is a bad combination. He felt very strongly about "no alcohol."

"We've discussed the wine issue," he said. "I thought we decided you were off wine indefinitely."

"We did, but I still don't see the point and I am resentful you won't even allow me one glass of wine. You are asking me to stop everything I like to do." I complained.

I slowly stopped drinking wine, except for an occasional glass here and there, but I did so very begrudgingly, as Ben and I continued therapy.

Ben and I had met another couple through one of Harold's Maggie Valley retreats. Cyndi and Ralph were both very sweet. She was the addict and Ralph was the fearful co-dependent. It was interesting to see the roles reversed and to be sitting in the same room going through all of our emotional shit together. There wasn't any cheating between them or in their marriage, so they had that going for them. I almost didn't know how to relate to married people who hadn't been cheated on. How sad is that?

Ben started off our group session saying that he was filled with fear and had been wanting to flee, to get separated. This, of course, caught me off guard and blew me away. I wanted to say, "Go ahead and try, who cares at this point?"

But that would be the old me, the one who couldn't control her anger. This was the new me, and I didn't say anything right away. When it was my turn to speak, I strongly told the group that I wouldn't buy into Ben's addict role and that I would detach from his retreat because it was founded in fear and not strength.

Harold had the two of us square off with one another, holding hands and staring into each others' eyes. For the first few minutes I smirked at him, knowing I'd called him out on his addict role, and he smirked back, knowing he had blind-sided me with his comment about wanting to separate. We were ridiculous at times.

"I am sometimes fearful of your rejection of me," Ben said. "And because I don't know what you'll say back to me, sometimes it is hard for me to use words of affirmation. The truth is, I would die for you if I could, if that would fix this. I am not going anywhere, and I am committed to do whatever it takes to get our relationship back on track."

While he was speaking, I cried. At the same time, I was thinking to myself that a similar declaration of my relationship like this would mean I could not rest easy on my day-dreams and fantasies of better men and better times. Ben wanted my compassion and spontaneity to return, my fun side to make another appearance in our lives. And I wanted my life back.

Later, Cyndi and I went for a hike and discussed Ben's sexual dysfunction and addiction. I think I freaked her out a bit talking about sexual addiction stuff. To be honest, I even scared myself a little, because I still felt like such a freak talking about all of this. I just couldn't believe this was my life that I was talking about and not someone else's.

We returned from the mountain retreat, and a few days later I was back in Harold's office listening to him read me the riot act for all my codependency issues, telling me I withdrew and turned into a doormat whenever Ben was around. He started in on the same old tune that my issues don't require a therapeutic week at some resort workshop, that what I needed was in-patient treatment at an honest-to-goodness trauma and depression facility. Harold was becoming a broken record.

Here we go again, I thought. I had just gotten back home and he wanted to send me away again! Well, I had news for him: Absolutely not! I'm the one driving around to meeting after meeting, trying to find peace with what my stupid, pervert husband had done to me. Because I couldn't forgive him for some things I considered unforgivable, Harold was saying I was the one who needed more treatment? No, I said. I was furious. And it didn't stop there. Here's what I wrote in my journal about it.

October 22, 1998

...I had to go into Ben's office this morning for a full
work up of tests—blood, urine, mammogram, the
whole nine yards. I'm still petrified I have AIDS.
I've got to walk the walk and have the courage to
change the things I can and the wisdom to know the
difference. Go get the tests and get rid of the fear,
Maurita, I kept telling myself. Done and done. Now,
wait for the results. Sure, no problem. In the meantime
I am sure I have AIDS.

No one, except maybe God, understands the agony
and terror I have felt about all this HIV stuff. Because
of Ben's rampant, hideous infidelity, 90 percent of it
without any form of protection, I always have to be
tested. Am worried what everyone is thinking when I
ask to be tested—they must know Ben is a cheat. I am
humiliated. I hate him for putting me through more
shit and pain. I have conversations in my head about
it. Let's face it, Maurita. You married one sick man.
How sick does that make you?

Three days later, the tests confirmed that I was perfectly
healthy. Another month of my daily routine went by with me
defending myself to Harold about Ben, staying off Ben when he
wanted sex, and trying to keep a handle on the kids. The walls in our
house had an echoing effect, and as soon as my voice reached a certain
volume, I heard it differently, and I knew I'd crossed a line. I really did
need to work on that part of my life where the kids were concerned,
especially because of my own family background.

Out of nowhere, or I thought it was out of nowhere, Ben
gave me a dozen roses and a nice note. I had forgotten it was our
anniversary. The first fourteen years of our marriage were dead to me.
That date only made me think back to my wedding day. It made me
want to cry when I thought of it. When I thought back on it, I found
myself wishing I could somehow go back, not marry him, and restart

the last sixteen years of my life. I didn't get Ben anything for our anniversary. Our marriage didn't mean anything but pain to me.

"Don't you think Ben made an honest effort to show you some affection?" Harold asked me later that week.

"Oh, give me a break. It's an effort to have sex, and the thought of that makes me physically ill," I told Harold. He thinks I am a loaded pistol and I'm hurting my marriage far more than I'm helping. What about me, I thought to myself. I'm the one with the nightmares, how about helping me with that? Where is God in all of this?

I tried to console my oldest daughter, who cried more often as she got older. Her fears and worries about Ben's behavior had grown as she matured. She should have been worrying about pimply boys and what to wear to the movies. Instead, she was upset about her Dad cheating on her mom. At times she was outright heartbroken about our family and at other times she became angry and resentful (a schedule not unlike my own), telling Ben she'd prefer it if he didn't go to her school for the high school basketball games. She was afraid her Dad will hit on one of the other moms in the stands. At the time, I thought she was kidding, but when her eyes started welling up, I pulled her into Harper's room and held her.

And where was Ben, the addict, through all of this? Not where he needed to be. He was off at a meeting, of course. He should have been fielding his daughter's questions and concerns, because it had been his decision to tell her about his sex addiction when she was far too young to understand it. I told him later that Ella was still having some serious issues and they should discuss their relationship, that he should be proactive instead of reactive. I am angry at myself for not protecting my little girl. She shouldn't have had to carry around the weight of his disclosure at that young age. Later, Ben and I got into it, snapping at each other.

"You're being cold and unresponsive and superior," I told Ben.

"I'm trying to protect myself and not let you take my inventory," he replied.

Take your thumb out of your mouth, you big baby, I wanted to yell right to his face. Wake up and smell the consequences of your actions.

On Harold's recommendation, we flew to sunny Scottsdale, Arizona, to attend our first Doctor's in Recovery weekend. For Ben, it was to meet new colleagues with similar struggles. I went there with such high hopes that I would finally meet another spouse of a sex addict. Ben was in a bad temper and acting out. He seemed to be at his worst when I was around, and vice versa. Lately, he'd been acting hyper and struggling, saying, "If only we had more sex, then I wouldn't be so jammed up." You big, fat sex addict, I thought to myself whenever he said that. I am no longer taking this personally, and your whining is finally falling on deaf ears.

After three meetings and two talks in Scottsdale, I was the only one who had stepped forward as the spouse of a sex addict.

On the way home from Scottsdale, after not finding a single spouse in the bunch I could relate to, I grew angry at Harold for assuring me I would meet other physicians' wives who were dealing with similar issues. I must be a freak of nature. There are no women who stay and put up with all of this emotional work and bullshit. I no longer wanted to deal with Ben's sexual addiction and go to meetings. I didn't want to be the poster wife for spouses of creeps. How humiliating that it had come to that. The only half-redeemable part of the trip came along when we spent some time in Sedona, Arizona.

If you don't believe in God or a Higher Power then visit Sedona. That place is absolutely gorgeous. We began to get a sense of perspective there. The world is a big place filled with a lot of people, and many people are dealing with far worse things than we are.

I sometimes forgot to count my blessings and the fact that my husband was sexually sober and healthy. I forget that I had four beautiful children and many nice things. Sedona, with its jutting red-faced cliffs and beautiful golden sunsets, was almost too much to take in all at once.

I thought I would take Harold up on his suggestion to get a spiritual mentor. Apparently, he had someone in mind for me already, and while I was not totally sold on the idea of adding another person to the long list of people who pitied me and my broken life, I was willing to try it if Harold thought it might help.

I continued going to church. I wrote about one Sunday in particular.

August, 1998

...Sunday morning I was in a bad mood. It was very hot and humid. I went to church and that kooky Scott Pyle sat down next to me! I even specifically picked the aisle seat and here he comes, with a big smile on his face. Now I am going to have to talk to him. Anyway, the testimony was good and the two songs were so moving. The forgiveness one was really incredible.

It was so clear that I was still struggling with this forgiveness issue. I just couldn't do it.

September 2, 1998

I never hear from Ben. He never calls. He shows back up at 9:45. I jump down his back the minute he walks through the door. We take the argument outside because Harper is still up and doesn't want to hear anymore fighting. We go to the pool area and I just let him have it. "Screw you," I'm yelling. "What do you have to say for yourself? I don't trust you worth a damn. How do I know that is where you've been this whole time?"

He was absolutely silent and finally said in a quiet, pompous, arrogant tone—get this—that I made him sick! How could I possibly doubt him at a time like this? I'll tell you how. You have lied to me hundreds of times about where you have been. "I was there for my best friend and his family," he was yelling. "Of course I didn't give you a second thought. Bill's father is laying there brain dead. I'm sorry I didn't think to call you."

I was so angry. I grabbed my keys and stormed out of the house. I drove in circles around Surfside for about an hour and a half. I crawled into bed an hour later and silently cried myself to sleep, waking up with puffy eyes.

"I think it's definitely time we have you meet with Gail," Harold said during our next session. "You can't keep putting Ben's recovery in the center of your life like that. You'll always end up shouting at one another. You need to make a spiritual connection and put that at the center of your life and your recovery. I want you to call Gail immediately."

"But she's the senior pastor's wife. What are we even going to talk about? I don't want to sit her down and tell her my whole sordid story. She's going to think I'm c;reepy," I told him.

"Call her today."

"All right," I sighed.

The first time we met, Gail Byrd gave me the first Bible I have ever owned. I was so nervous ringing her doorbell, because we had never before met. This woman, the pastor's wife, was about to know everything about me. It was nerve-wracking. At about five-feet-seven and on the thin side with shoulder-length dark brown hair and beautiful dark brown eyes, she looked perfectly put together. She has the greatest looking teeth and smile. Her voice, that of a real Southerner, was quiet and calming.

We walked down the street from her house to the beach, and walked up and down the shore, her listening and me talking in circles around Ben's disease and my continued brokenness. I cried intermittently, talking of Tucson and On-Site and continually failing to find God's help.

"I don't know what else to do. I just give up, Gail. I just want to give up," I told her.

She asked if I wanted Jesus Christ to come into my life, and I wept and said, "Yes, where else am I going to go?"

She prayed for me, right there on the beach. That moment with Gail was a huge breakthrough for me, because I had never publicly talked about Jesus or my faith.

"Dear Lord, come to the aid of your daughter, Maurita," she said. "Find your way into her heart and bring her strength and peace."

We walked back to her house and made plans to meet once a week. The entire next day I felt drained, yet I also felt as if I'd really begun making huge strides. Gail was fantastic.

"I'm glad you're so excited about Gail," Harold said.

"I am," I said. "I feel like I am in for a lot more work ahead of me. I don't know that much about Jesus or the Bible, and I certainly don't know what a personal relationship with Christ means, really. But I am really determined to follow through with this."

"I want you to stay connected to Gail. It's like I always say, Mo, I'll be happy to sit here once a week for twenty years and take your money, but I can only guide you back to the path you've lost. I can't get in there and fix your heart—only you and God can do that."

"I know, I know. I have to have God as my greatest happiness, my center. Not Ben."

I felt like some evangelist, some kind of holy roller. I didn't have the strength of conviction to proclaim things like that without lowering my voice. Fortunately, I had no problem reading the Bible that Gail gave me; it had a great table of contents that listed specific topics like anger, rage, and depression with accompanying Bible verses. My first assignments were to read the story of Job. I read that a couple of times and some of the verses dealing with self-esteem.

I met with Gail regularly. She was really incredible. I almost cried every time we talked. She was forceful yet gentle and compassionate. I let my fat ego and my arrogance shine through and she called me on it, but in a loving way.

I tended to view myself as how I thought other people were thinking of me. I came across quotes that said, "When God becomes important to us, his view of us will supersede all others." What a freeing concept that was. I began to realize that it was possible to live my life as God viewed me.

My parents had long planned to renew their vows—a symbolic gesture that I held out hope for Ben and me doing someday. But lately, it felt like we'd be celebrating ten glorious years of being divorced before we celebrated twenty-five years of being married. We were taking our marriage one day at a time. Having Gail in my corner and having her help me to call on God during my times of need instead of blasting Ben was beginning to make a difference in our daily lives.

September, 1998. Vermont

It was a quiet and religious ceremony in my parents' church in Ludlow. My father wept reciting his vows, and my mother got a little teary eyed too. I was beginning to wonder if she had the capacity to let loose anymore, to have her emotions actually show. I cry all the time; I even cry at TV commercials. I don't know which is better. The priest who presided over their original wedding day was there for their vow renewal too. He was very old and didn't say anything, but he made it. That was really neat.

After communion, my father said a few words, very Dad–like, with funny anecdotes about my mother. When he finished, my mother thanked everyone for coming, very Mom-like.

The party moved back to my parents' home where a beautiful catered dinner was waiting. After dinner, before the cake, I stood up and gave a toast to my parents. I told them how thankful I was to have them as my parents and how wonderful they have been in their support of me in dealing with my husband's addictions. I said, "I just want everyone here to know how much I love them." Then I walked over to where they were standing and cupped my hands around their faces and gave them each a kiss. There wasn't a dry eye in the house.

My sisters didn't say anything.

My brother, David, with Mike by his side, also remained quiet during the toasts, and justifiably so.

My forty-third birthday snuck around the corner and landed flat in my lap. I felt scared, old, battered and tired. Harold thought that, even with Gail's help, I couldn't oust Ben from the center of my life and that keeping him there was poisoning everything else.

Gail was relentless and, thankfully, never gave up on me. The week surrounding my birthday, I felt really down and I wanted so badly to cancel our weekly meeting. I even picked up the phone a couple of times, but the butterflies in my stomach where churning so that I couldn't bring myself to call her. Instead, I prayed. "God, please give me the strength to follow through. Give me the strength to face Gail every week, and not give up on what it is You want me to do."

I am beginning to think that those butterflies are now taking up permanent residence in my stomach. I imagine most people only feel them once in a while, but mine had been active and angry for years. I wished they would fly away.

Chapter Ten. A New Low

છ૭૮૩

I had been doing a lot of reading, mostly books by Melody
Beattie and Marianne Williamson. I love the way they both write.
Melody gets right to the point and Marianne is very soothing. I was
waiting for Gail and getting ready to have one of our meetings when I
came across this great piece written by Marianne:

> One Woman, who has really been through it, meets
> another Woman, who has really been through it, and
> together they enter a new dimension of Awareness.
> More and More, we Woman are no longer interested in
> getting together just to whine and pity. We're ready to
> be in the presence of Others who have not just fallen,
> but have learned to get back up. Who have not just
> failed, but have learned from the failure. Who have
> not just lost, but have reached for the personal success
> involved in handling loss with Dignity and Grace.

Fantastic. Someday I am going to be that woman, I thought, as
I tore it out of the magazine and glued it on to Melody Beattie's book,
The Language of Letting Go.

Gail is a wise woman, one who knows there is darkness and
light, who truly believes in miracles. I had to get the courage to keep
showing up to face her.

Right before Gail arrived at the beach house, Ben called. He
had just finished up a grueling session with Harold and had to sign an
abstinence contract.

"I'm not allowed to masturbate, and we're encouraged not
to have sex," he told me. "He thinks that we hide behind it, use it
against each other, and never really engage each other intimately in a
nonsexual way."

"I actually don't disagree with that." I said. "It is such a creepy thing to sign, though."

Gail showed up right after we hung up, and I told her about the new abstinence contract. I always felt I might be offending her when I shared those types of intimate details. My marriage seemed so dysfunctional compared with hers, and I often wondered what she thought of me. I also tended to use profanity, so having Gail around was helping with that.

After going over the reading materials and assignments she had given me for that week, I launched into something that had been really bothering me. It was about my quest to bring God into my life.

"Where was He when my dickhead husband called me and broke my heart into a million pieces and left it lying on the floor?" I asked her.

"Well, that's a little bit selfish, isn't it?" Gail asked. "Had you been praying that day, asking for His help, asking for His strength? And I will tell you where He was. He was with you the entire time. He was heartbroken for you and with you long before you knew of Ben's deceits."

It was incredibly tough to take something as far gone as my life and recenter it with something I didn't fully understand. I told Gail that and she agreed it would take a lot more time and dedication than I thought it would, which only made me feel more lost. My addiction to Ben encouraged me to put him at the center of my life, but my anger toward Ben encouraged me to put myself first. Now I had Gail and her husband, Ronnie, urging me to focus my life on God and surrender my pain to a Higher Power.

October 17, 1999

…Ben and I may finally be turning a corner. I am feeling less anger, disgust, and sadness and more hopeful and loving. I am also learning—very slowly—how to let myself be vulnerable to him. Had a good session with Harold yesterday. I told him I had been wrong all these years when I thought I was an OK, moral person. Through reading the Bible and working

with Gail—I am finding I am a big sinner and have
been pretty ugly and a shit head too. Harold broke out
in a big smile and said he has been trying to tell me
that for two years—in a more loving way of course!

October 18, 1999

I have been getting along better with Ben. I really
do appreciate the efforts he is making to be loving
and kind to me. He is getting more vocal about
complimenting me. I am now at the point where I can
accept compliments from him instead of brushing him
off or saying something sarcastic back to hurt him.

Ben and I were planning to attend a retreat in Maggie Valley
with Cyndi and Ralph and another couple I didn't know. A few days
before this retreat, we had been at one of Henry's soccer games. Ben's
eyes kept focused on a cute young mom wearing dopey soccer ball
earrings. He gawked so long and so hard, I was surprised he knew the
score of the game. I wasn't trying to be malicious about it, but it was
definitely something I wanted to explore in group therapy.

Before we even got past check-in at the retreat, Ben went on
for ten minutes about he wasn't making progress because he has issues
with his inner child and showing his feelings.

I didn't say anything, but I thought, *Cry me a fucking river.*

I wasn't in a good place after that, so it was good that I had
learned to control my jabs and barbs, keeping my inappropriate
comments to myself. Ben told the group that he felt strangled by my
codependency and my neediness and that he felt like he was stepping
into a cage when he entered our home.

"I hope someday when Maurita gets healthier, that she decides
I am not what she wants, and that we have the courage to end our
marriage and go our separate ways," he told them.

Again, my thoughts weren't nice ones. I thought, *I hope I have
the courage to punch you in your puffy, arrogant face.* Courage? What the
hell did Ben know about courage? I was so angry.

After the group session, we played whiffle ball, with the wives versus the husbands. I nailed Ben twice in the back running to first base.

"I'm not going to stand around and watch you bring Ben down with your resentment and angry spirit," Harold said a week later. "Your attitude toward your husband is terrible. Do you realize how you are treating him?"

"Me?" I asked. "I'm the one who has to bury the sex addict shit every meeting I go to. I think that is why this is so hard for me. Progress, not perfection. Isn't that what you always say?"

I broke down and cried in his office, something I hated to do after all this time. I hated feeling so vulnerable in front of Harold. It was humiliating. Eventually, the session ended and I drove aimlessly around town for a while, not wanting to go home.

During this time, we were also having huge financial problems, and Harold was after me to get my resume out of mothballs and find a job. I had quit working when I got pregnant with Ella and we moved to Myrtle Beach, so it had been fifteen years since I had been in the business world. I had wanted to make a go of painting furniture and accessories, but that was not going well.

My priorities about what I wanted to do with my life had shifted. I decided to call on one of my favorite teachers from Coastal Carolina University, where I finished my degree. He was glad to hear from me, and we met in his campus office to discuss my future. Eddie Dyer, tall and lanky, with kind eyes and a smile, had a laidback personality. He was a lawyer by training with a solid reputation across the state. He also taught political science courses, which is how I met him. I didn't tell him much about Ben, except that he gone through rehab for a drug problem. I told him I needed a job.

He asked me what I thought I wanted to do, and I said I was stuck about whether to open my own studio to be a full-time painter or going back to school to become a lawyer.

He said, "What is stopping you from taking the LSAT?"

I said that I was afraid to try, because I did so poorly on my SAT in high school.

He smiled a little and said, "When did you take your SAT?"

"When I was sixteen," I answered.

"You're how old now?"

"I'm forty-three."

"Do you mean to tell me that you have based your adult career possibilities on a test you took twenty-seven years ago?" he asked.

A little light bulb went off in my head. "Yes, I guess I have."

He was right, of course.

Then he said something I'll always remember. "I have had hundreds of students over the years and you come to mind as one of the top fifty."

Then he said, "For the next thirty days, wake up every morning like you were either going to a law office or walking into a studio. Go through in your mind what you think you are preparing for in your day, what that day will look like. Take the financial concern completely out of it, like you are independently wealthy. If it is law school, call me back."

I went home and did what he suggested. After three days of visualizing getting dressed in a suit each day, being stuck in an office, having to work my way up to handling the kinds of cases I would want, and having to deal with men in a courtroom with zero integrity, I did not see myself as a lawyer. My creative side won out. It was a big realization.

Eddie's comment about how I had based my future on a test I took when I was a kid really hit home. I was very encouraged that a man of his stature said I was bright and capable of doing anything I put my mind to. Oh, how I wish I had had a teacher like him in my corner during high school.

In the meantime, Ben and I continued to work on our respective recoveries.

October, 1999

...Ben is turning into a golf freak. He did tell me his sex drive has really toned down because of his break in exercise. I don't want him to pork out, but I sure as hell don't want him relapsing back into his sick behaviors. Went to Al-Anon and that was good— talked about the Seventh Step. I have been happier lately and I attribute that to establishing a relationship with Gail. My dependency on Harold has decreased since I have started seeing Gail. Now I have Gail to share my daily struggle and fear with. How lucky I am! Also, I am beginning to have more of an interest in focusing on making me a better person rather than focusing on Ben.

October 31, 1999

…Out of nowhere, on Halloween, Ben got baptized. Ronnie was already performing two other baptisms when he asked if anyone else would like to be baptized. Scott encouraged Ben to take the plunge, so Ben said yes. Harold came and stood next to me, watching this incredible moment. Afterward, we all hugged and cried and some of us went out to lunch. Sometimes my life feels like a dream.

After Ben got baptized, the days fell off the calendar like autumn leaves. It felt like one minute I'd be walking the path with Gail, searching my soul and readying a place for Jesus in my heart, and the next minute Ben and I were laughing about nonsense with the kids laughing right along with us.

Then, one Tuesday, my husband remembered it was our wedding anniversary. He surprised me with an empty beach house lit with candles. Sitting in the middle of the room was our massage table from the house. There was incense burning, my favorite music, and a nice bottle of wine. We went out to the porch and had cheese and crackers and talked. We decided that the people who we were on our wedding day were dead. They'd lived a life somewhere else, and that life had ended. We were living a new life, and it was a new and difficult one, but we were willing to keep trying.

We agreed to call this a celebration of being together now. I went inside and took off my clothes and Ben gave me a great massage. For an hour, we didn't talk, and his hands felt so strong and soothing as he massaged my back and arms. We went into the bedroom together. He had lighted candles and made up the bed with fresh linen. We made love to each other—slowly and openly and lovingly. The way it should be done between a husband and wife who love each other. It was incredible.

November 24, 1999

…Last night was awesome. After we had sex, I took a shower, and Ben went to the store and bought food to make dinner. He made a great pasta dinner. I felt so relaxed and happy—I didn't want the night to end. I felt for the first time, I think maybe ever, that I felt his love for me in my soul.

…Went to Al-Anon and was glad I went. Two new people were there—a really pretty lady that Harold wanted me to meet and someone else. I shared about humility, humbleness, and infidelity.

December 1, 1999

…I am really struggling right now. I am depressed and constantly in fantasyland. I don't get it because I felt so good and hopeful last week. I feel I have forgiven Ben, but I still grapple with despair and sadness. I feel my tendency to withdraw from people is coming back. I am avoiding our new Bible study tonight. I am uncomfortable with the dinner part because the food stinks. The Bible stuff is interesting but goes on about ten minutes too long. Everyone in our group is sweet. Ben falls asleep about ten minutes into the tape so I sit there resentful because he isn't paying any attention, and we are only there because he insisted on signing us up. I feel like clamming up and having nothing to do with anyone.

…I am resentful of all of this recovery stuff. I always feel I should be doing something else. Actually, I would love to devote an hour a day to reading and studying, but it seems impossible.

December 12, 1999

It is Sunday night, and it was a real disaster of a day. I am choked by my children and husband and feel trapped and powerless when I am with them altogether. It still feels hideous for me to go out in public with Ben. He is indifferent and sleeps through half the day. I grow restless and overwhelmed as the day wears on. Family days are something I endure and really can't stand doing.

December 20, 1999

…What a disastrous morning. My temper and screaming are terrible, and I lost control with Ella. It's only a few hours later now and I can't even remember what set me off, but there I went. I went after her in the kitchen and went to kick her in the butt, thank goodness I barely connected.

…Then Ben comes downstairs in the midst of all this chaos, screaming his head off, holding my shoulders and pushing me away, screaming that I was out of control. Ella was crying so hard, so hurt by what I had done and my yelling. What a mess. I started crying, grabbed some of my stuff and fled to the beach house.

…I feel so empty. I am a horrible mother. But I am afraid the damage is already done.

I think I lashed out at Ella when I saw her acting like she wasn't good enough. When I see her insecurity, her feelings of inadequacy, it's like I see myself, and I want to jar her out of it before she slides into a life … like mine. I hated myself and I hated Ben too.

I called Harold from the beach house, and he advised me to stay put for a while, calm down, journal about what had happened, then go back home and make amends to the kids and Ben. I listened to his advice and felt much calmer, although shame and guilt about my behavior lingered like a dark cloud over me.

Eventually, I did go back to the house and apologize to Ella and Henry for having to deal with the chaos and fallout of sexual addiction in their parents' lives.

I overhead Henry ask Ella, "Do you still hate Mom?"

How could I feel any worse? There had to be something of value—something to be gained by experiencing the badness that is now a part of my life. I had experienced pain, trauma, broken heart, broken spirit, loss, grief, fear, embarrassment, humiliation, mean-spiritedness, betrayal, seeing anguish and fear in my children's faces, and depression. My physical symptoms included constipation, nausea, hemorrhoids, loss of my menstrual period for three months, hair loss, weight loss, and inability to sleep.

It was close to Christmas and instead of singing carols and smiling together, our family spent its time going from room to room apologizing to one another for various outbursts of anger. When I spoke to Olivia and Harper, they told me they'd been watching me cry for two years, and they were worried I was going to kill myself.

So, one of my New Year's resolutions in 2000 was to get a grip on my anger and to keep my crying under control around the kids.

January 2, 2000

This is my first journal entry of the New Year. Spent New Year's Eve at the Pyle's house. Had a really nice time. All the kids came too. I made a cake. We left about 11:15 and got home in time to watch the ball drop in Times Square. On New Year's Day I made a really nice family brunch—muffins, roast beef, the whole thing. Ben is a couch potato and self-absorbed.

January 10, 2000

…On Sunday morning we woke up early and had a good frank discussion. I learned some new things about Ben. Henry fell off the banister and landed on my china buffet, broke my new favorite vase, knocked over a dozen roses, and water is now soaking into my favorite books. I didn't get mad though because, thank goodness, he didn't get hurt. Ben is resentful that I am a lousy cook and says I make him feel like a failure every time he walks into the house. I have mixed feelings about some of his resentments, especially the cooking one. I really don't give two shits about that. Let him cook his own dinner if he doesn't like mine.

January 16, 2000

Ben and I are just OK. He is a little restless and having problems staying away from porn on the Internet. I will no longer allow him to criticize the family scene at home as he puts such little input into it. I told him he was like a guy who complains about government but does not vote.

A winter snowstorm rolled through in late January. We woke up to a beautiful snowfall. We got at least five or six inches. The kids were thrilled. Olivia and Harper were dressed by 6:30 in the morning and outside playing. Ella was unimpressed and slept until 10 A.M. It was fun watching the dogs playing in the snow. Even old man Herbie bounced around with a bit of a spring in his step.

I had been angry about money. It seemed to rule and ruin every day. We had paid so much in therapy between Ben and me, that it would have been cheaper at that point to buy Harold and have him live in our house. I hated being home. I hated our house. I would have talked to Gail, but she had gone out of town. I had just Ben, and he was still just Ben. We had our good days and our bad days, but we seemed to be having more bad ones.

February 1, 2000

I have hit bottom. Had kind of a migraine all day today. Henry is sick as shit—stayed home and threw up and slept all day. He scares me when he is sick because he is so little and vulnerable looking when he doesn't feel well. Went to Al-Anon and the subject was anger—perfect for me because that is all I feel lately. I feel smothered and need a break.

February 8, 2000

...Ben and I are distant. Woke up early and he told me he had a masturbation slip on Monday. He did it when he was home alone. His therapy group really got on him about his poor relationships with his three daughters and his petty resentments at me—not to mention the slip. He even made one of the girls in the group cry because of his sarcastic comments to her. Listening to him made me feel sad for him; he finally let other people see the ugly side of him. As he got out of bed, I very gently asked him to tell me when and what he was resentful of, and how I wished he would open up to me more. So he promptly got out of bed, turned his back to me, pulled his boxer's down, pulled his butt apart, and mooned me! He is so gross—that was his version of opening up to me. What a dick—I looked away because this is just not funny anymore. How sad. He is so pathetically disrespectful to himself, our relationship, and me.

As soon as Gail came back in town, I unloaded to her about God not listening and not helping me. I told her that no matter what I did, nothing changed. I told her that the dullness in my soul was as listless as Ben on the sofa at night.

A couple of nights later I sat out at the pool area with Tucson and a glass of wine. I was in an awful mood. I reflected on how great I'd felt that day after Al-Anon but how short-lived those feelings were.

I felt great again after my session with Harold, but those feelings also subsided quickly. The beach house gave me another spike of happiness when I had the house all to myself for the afternoon. But even then, I would realize I'd have to go back to my dirty house with my silly husband snoring all night and waking me up in the morning to talk about masturbating. I didn't know what to do about it anymore. Any of it.

Soon after, Ben left for a week at On-site, and I was happy to see him go. I didn't need to analyze what my feelings meant.

"It means that you're happier when he's not around. Why is that?"Harold asked.

"It means I'm happier when he's not around because I feel like he is a reminder of my pain. He is a reminder of so many things that are wrong in my life."

I knew where he was going with this. I still had not ousted Ben from the center of my life and when I got angry with him or with myself, it was because I was not putting my faith in God, or even myself.

"I know we've been over it before. I'm so tired, just so tired," I said to him.

Harold made me do a Gratitude List right there in the office, even though I felt lousy. I was grateful for my health, for Ben being healthy, sober, and working, for old man Herbie, and for the kids' health.

Compiling the list took a shorter time than I thought it would. Then I added another item to the list—a cool new camera so I could take Henry's soccer pictures. As usual, I had a lot to be grateful for.

When Ben came home from On-site he looked refreshed. We put the kids to bed and sat at the table and discussed his week.

April 15, 2000

Ben had an OK time and developed some new insights from his week at On-site. He didn't crack up or feel any grief. He worked on his codependency issues related to me. I just wish he would leave and end this misery. My feelings for him are dead. I love him

for the children we have and when I see glimpses of
the man he could be, but my feelings are mostly of
hostility and nothingness. I am in a bad mood, because
our marriage sucks and my house is a mess. One of
my dogs is dying, the other one is getting fat, mean,
and out of control. Great.

The funniest thing happened today. Olivia's guinea
pig, Carmel Corn had two babies—little, black, slug-
like things with rollie-pollie eyes. We didn't know
she was pregnant. Olivia called all her friends on the
phone, excited to share the news. I overheard Olivia
say, somewhat exasperated, "Well, I don't know how it
happened. All I know is that I'm a grandmother."

Ha! Sweet little Olivia and her joyful innocence saved
the day. I will smile to myself for years to come each
time I think of her saying that.

While Ben was at On-site, he revealed some truly serious lost
emotions from his childhood. The therapists wanted him to pursue
these feelings when he got home with Harold. They urged him to
involve his parents to uncover more in-depth family history.

It turns out that Ben's parents had been raised in emotionally
abusive households. His grandfather had beat his Dad, and his
mother's father had hit her. One of his grandparents had had a long-
term affair, and Ben's dad had an affair as well. From there, Ben
confessed he'd been deeply hurt when he was put in the middle of his
father's affair during Ben's college years. Ben had covered for his Dad
on one or two occasions.

"Forget Ben," Harold told me. "Forget it. What about when
you were slapped around as a kid? What about that?"

"Well, yeah, I know. But, I still can't help feeling a little sorry
for him," I said.

Harold laid it on thick that day, telling me that I was still
putting Ben's feelings ahead of my own and expecting more from Ben

then I give. Harold said I was clingy and still too wrapped up in Ben's life, his behavior, his feelings.

"You're still living your life through Ben," Harold said.

"Ouch," I replied.

May 14, 2000. Mother's Day

…I feel kind of funny about Mother's Day because I haven't been a very good mother since getting into recovery. I have been very self-absorbed in my own pain and agony, and I have really short-changed the kids. I have been so caught up in my own world that I have cut them out of healthy, motherly love. I am not feeling good about myself today. Plus, I have a $700 Amex bill that I can't afford to pay, and I'll have to show it to Ben.

Just when you think that the frayed rope that is your life has started braiding itself together again, just when you rediscover that swimming in the open waves makes you feel like a child again, a friend goes into massive heart failure, and your thirteen-year-old son tells you he is experimenting with pot. Happy Mother's Day, Maurita!

Because of recovery, Jenny came into our lives. She was a beautiful person, inside and out, who got into recovery and befriended us. She met Ben at a meeting. We didn't know each other well until that point. I always thought she had such a great life. I was wrong. Jenny was battling her own demons and finally went into recovery about two years after Ben did. We got to know her and began hanging out with her and her husband. She embraced her new life and was fun to be around.

One evening, a group of us went to an open AA meeting to watch a mutual good friend, Charlie, pick up his two-year chip. Jenny sat next to me. We all went out to dinner afterward and had a great time. Jenny had a heart attack the very next day. I couldn't believe it. She seemed so healthy, so strong and vibrant.

They put her in the Cardiac ICU and she started going downhill. They sent her to a teaching hospital after she had complications. She got her heart condition under control only to be told she had liver cancer.

Other storm clouds were building over my head. I thought it was a freak occurrence that a vibrant person like Jenny would have a heart attack. It turned out that this was just the first domino in the line to go down.

The next morning, I woke up to find that old man Herbie had shit all over the place. It was painfully obvious to Ben and me that Herbie had had enough of this life and needed to be put out of his misery.

"I can't face this. It's too much for me right now," Ben said.

"OK. I'll take Herbie in to be put down," I said, sadly. Harper and I loaded Herbie into the car and drove slowly, crying the whole way to the veterinary office. We both kissed our beloved pet on his nose and left him in compassionate hands to find his own peace. It could not have been easy being our dog. I hope we gave him a good life.

July 8, 2000

Jenny's last two months of health problems were
incredible and mind-boggling. It should be a lesson
to me and everyone else how fortunate and fragile
we are. Instead, I allow myself to get sucked up in my
self-pity and petty bullshit life.

In the middle of all this, Harold decides he won't see us as a couple any longer and recommends some guy named Stuart. Stuart has a kinder, gentler approach to therapy. I would really prefer not to start anything as big as marriage counseling over again, especially with a new therapist.

Days later, I finally broke down and told my Al-Anon meeting about Ben's sexual addiction. In doing so, I met this grandmotherly type woman whose husband had sex addiction problems with pornography. Finally, I remembered thinking, a spouse to talk to. I rushed to Harold's to tell him the news and found that he and Ben were both there to tell me that I needed to go to in-patient treatment immediately.

Fuck Ben. Fuck Harold.

I had a trip planned to California with Ella and Harper, and I was not missing it. I'd already promised it to them, and my broken promises to my children had to stop.

When we got home, Ben told the girls that their mother was headed off for treatment for a couple of weeks. They, of course, were upset, because whenever I was not around, their Dad completely ignored them.

"Can we hire a full-time mother while you're away?" they asked me.

You already have a full-time mother, I thought to myself. Eat shit Ben. I'm not going anywhere. Little did I know, Ben had already spoken to all the kids about my anger and depression problems and told them that if I didn't go into in-patient treatment—if I went to California instead—then he would be taking them and leaving the house.

He was now officially out of his mind, I thought. When I heard about it, I blew my stack. I followed Ben around the house, seething and yelling. He finally stomped off to the downstairs bedroom and started watching TV.

I tried to sleep upstairs. At 11 o'clock I went downstairs only to find Ben lying in our bedroom, watching TV, and eating string licorice.

"This isn't over," I said to him.

"It is over. You're going to get help," he said. "If Harold wants you to go to in-patient treatment, then you're going."

"Who the fuck do you think you are?" I yelled. I ripped the covers off of him and took his candy and threw it against the wall. He got out of bed, and I hauled off and punched him as hard as I could in his arm.

"Honeyeeee," he said, his teeth clenched.

"Beeeeen," I seethed back.

He didn't say anything. Instead, he got dressed, left the

room, and headed toward the study. I followed him, yelling various things at him.

"You'll never make my decisions again," I hollered. "How could you use the kids against me? How could you do that to me after everything I have done for you? After all the pain that your sick fucking lifestyle has caused this family?" I had no reason to believe that our four children, blessed with perfect hearing, were not awake, huddling together upstairs, listening, and scared. My rage was selfish, and I was unconcerned about where the fallout landed.

"That's it," he yelled back. He pulled two suitcases from the closet, opened them, then put them on the floor. He pointed at them and said, "You're leaving, and you're leaving tonight!"

"Oh no I'm not. I'm not going anywhere." I pushed him against the wall. He pushed back and I almost lost my footing. Ben went to the bedroom and dialed 911.

"We're having a domestic dispute, and maybe it's a good idea for you to send over an officer," he told dispatch. He gave them our address. Stunned that he actually called the police, I tried to calm the kids as best I could. Then I walked out the front door and sat on the steps to wait for the police. Five minutes later, two police cars pulled up, and I thanked God that they didn't have their lights on as they drove through our neighborhood. I walked to one of the cars and the officer immediately asked me, "Is there any alcohol, drugs, or weapons involved here?"

"No," I answered. "I can't believe my husband called you for this. We were having an argument over a trip I am taking. He is just a control freak." That's when Ben emerged from the house with his cell phone in his hand.

One of the officers looked at Ben and asked me if that is the doctor who swims. I answered, "Yeah, that's him all right, the nut case."

"I'm on an emergency call to our therapist," he told the officers, who stayed in their cars. When it was apparent that the conflict was nonthreatening, one car left. One of the remaining officers called Ben over to the police car, where I was standing. He said that unless one of us was pressing charges, they would have to say goodnight. He said it was not against the law to argue with a spouse.

Ben handed me the phone, which was still connected to Harold.

"Hey, Mo. How are you?" he calmly asked.

"How do you think I am doing? The frigging police are in my front yard right now telling me that one of us has to press charges or they're leaving," I told him.

"The police, huh?"

"Yes. The police."

"Have you had enough of the craziness in your life? Are you ready to get out of the environment you are living in?" Harold asked, then paused. It was the calmest silence I'd ever heard, and I could hear myself breathing. My heart continued to race as I stood there in my front yard in the middle of the night, watching the police pull away.

"Yes," was all I said.

I ran back inside and up the stairs to find all four of the kids huddled together on Harper's bed. I was horrified at what had just happened, what these four kids had just witnessed. I tried to reassure them as best I could that we all were going to be OK. Ben came in, and we said a family prayer together. Ben slept in Henry's room and Olivia slept with me. She was so upset and confused by what had just happened. At that moment, I hated Ben's guts.

The next morning, he got up and wanted to know if I wanted anything for breakfast, as if nothing huge had happened the night before. What a nut case.

July 2000

...I was pretty numb all day and went about my business as well as could be expected. We went to see a movie as a family. I made an appointment with Harold last night. That session really helped me. He told me that there was a strong possibility a divorce would happen. He said Ben was a sick man and he really didn't know any other woman who would put up with what I have put up with. He is right. He gave me his full support about going to treatment at the "crazy Meadows," as I called it.

ೞೞ

Part Three: Healing

ೞೞ

Chapter Eleven. Getting Over Myself

ℰℭ

I'd been to the Scottsdale area before, but this time I was filled with apprehension about the weeks ahead. Yet, a part of me was relieved to be away from Ben. Olivia was too young to understand what was going on. Henry and Harper thought I had a problem with depression and crying too much, and only Ella knew about the sexual infidelity.

August 11, 2000

…I did manage to talk to my father on the phone yesterday, and I was somewhat surprised by him. My father, the devout Catholic, told me that divorce was not the worst thing that could happen. I promised him that this was it, and if I still felt this way about my marriage after Arizona, then I would divorce Ben. The end had finally come. I can't bring myself to talk to my close friends or siblings before I leave or I will freak out and lose my nerve to get on that plane. I know they would tell me to dump this loser before he does any more damage…

The following journal entries are centered around my experience in a full-fledged, five-week, in-patient treatment facility. The Meadows is the real deal—serious treatment. For those of you who may be thinking about the same kind of in-depth treatment, the following is what this experience was like for me. I view the time I spent at the Meadows as one of the defining chapters of my recovery journey. I finally got off the fence and felt, from my heart, that I wanted my husband and family back.

August 17, 2000

...Dear Me. Oh my God! Here I sit on my patio outside my room overlooking the mountains of Wickenburg, Arizona. How did I get here? I made it here Sunday night at 11:15 p.m. I was so tired and drained from the day and flight. Leaving was so hard to do. I cried when I said good-bye to the kids, and I wept a little when I said good-bye to the husband at the airport. I think I was numb and joyless the whole trip. Some guy in a van picked me up and drove me here. Then my nightmare began. When I arrived it was hot and my driver took all my stuff right into the nurse's station. I sat there shell-shocked as they began to check everything I brought.

I had to pee in a cup to check for drugs, followed by a new patient work-up, which lasted about an hour. With all the bullshit and paperwork and going through all my stuff and clothes pockets, I didn't get to bed until 5 A.M.

They woke me up at 6:15 A.M. for fucking blood work. I was a basket case. I felt like a convicted felon. All I did was cry when someone talked to me. I am just a doctor's wife from Myrtle Beach—how did I wind up here? There are some really sick looking people here, including people detoxing from serious drug problems. I kept saying, "I want to go home."

...endless trips to the nurses' station for blood pressure checks and "feelings checks." Doctor appointments every day for three days. My tiny room with no privacy, combined with having to be under the watchful eye of the nurses' station was indescribable. My phone calls to Ben and the kids were awful. All I did was cry and tell them how horrible it was, and how I wanted to come home. Ben was sweet and supportive—told me to give it a couple of days before I made any decisions. Oh, they made me call him at 4 A.M. Myrtle Beach time to tell him that my payment was not set up right. What a racket!

…By yesterday morning I really wanted to get the fuck out of acute care and move into a dormitory style place for women. It was bullshit when the morning nurse said I could move upon availability, so I brought that up at the morning peer meeting. I had to go see a shrink and that went OK. He gave me his go-ahead to move off the unit, so off I went. I made my own bed and couldn't believe it, because I got the room of my dreams. I have the front room with access to a sliding glass door and patio.

Eventually I resigned myself to the idea that I was in treatment, and I felt ready to do what is necessary to get a healthy mindset and lifestyle. I held my first COSA (for spouses of sex addicts) meeting and two women showed up. I was taking some initiative and responsibility in my program. I was making the best of my situation.

August 19, 2000

…What an incredible day. Trying to stay in the moment is difficult. Was a little overwhelmed with all the information my main therapist told me. I had to do my autobiography today, and I had to list all the things and events that keep playing over and over in my head that were painful, shameful, or humiliating. Mentioned some incidents in childhood—especially with my mother, the assault by a bunch of lifeguards one summer at Morse's Pond where I taught swimming, that creepy next door neighbor, and five or six events in dealing with Ben's sexual disclosure and the first year of discovery.

....Well, guess what? Harold was right, again. I am suffering from post-traumatic stress disorder from childhood and my marriage! My therapist made me describe in detail the day I got grabbed into the boy's locker room at work and was held down and finger-painted, while I was wearing a bikini. He called that a definite sexual assault, and if it had been taken seriously at the time it happened, those boys would have been arrested. I also described in detail the exploits of one of my neighbors when I was probably eight or ten and he was sixteen or seventeen. I just thought he was a pervert but harmless. My therapist helped me see it was a definite form of sexual abuse. Surprise! I am tired and drained.

August 22, 2000

...So far today, I feel kind of bummed out. I am very lonely and I have so much on my mind. It is becoming so clear to me that I have carried around so much shame from my past, but also shame from my life with Ben. I am so ashamed I picked him for my mate and I let him treat me the way he has.

August 24, 2000

...This week is inner child week. I will do my stuff tomorrow. Week going fast. Have to admit Ben has been great on the phone. He should be. I chaired a great group tonight. I brought the new betrayal book that I found at the bookstore with me and we read from it—all the pages are great. Some very frank and open discussions about trust and why we stay. One new woman had been with her husband for three years after he disclosed, too—but he had relapsed a couple of times and even gave her a STD. Talk about betrayal. And, another woman is really struggling. Her husband just disclosed to her about his prostitution addiction and she tried to kill herself a few days later.

August 25, 2000

...I need to get my emotions in check. I just finished "Inner Child week" and I am so drained. I have a lot of sadness and grief tied up inside me and it came out today. I said a lot of the things that I needed to say. I was really able to access my grief and make contact with my inner child. As stupid as this shit sounds, it was really easy to see myself as a little girl.

August 26, 2000

...Here I sit out at the pool feeling very old. Am talking to a nineteen-year-old about her crazy drug habits. Next, I sat with a woman from the COSA group. She is sweating out her blood test results for STDs. I know how she feels. She is so angry and scared.

...I am finding out I am a "rager." I take my anger to an inappropriate level called rage. I didn't know rage was a major category you need to seek recovery for. Had a fun dinner. Sat with some of the sex addict men. I really like them; they are for the most part really nice guys. They are just so sick in that one area of their lives. I wish I could feel the compassion I have for them with my own husband.

...Oh, most of the people here are on some kind of medication so I realize I have to tread lightly and give people their space. I have learned so much so far, and I am looking forward to this week which is spirituality week. Then I can't wait to face my family and make amends and accept responsibility for my behavior.

August 28, 2000

My phone conversation with Ben was good. He said
he has a new appreciation for what I do all day. The
girls were difficult because Harper started crying as
soon as she heard my voice, and I guess Olivia caught
the fever. So, she started crying too. I felt terrible and
helpless when I hung up the phone.

...My friend here is going through a real shit time. Her
husband's sexual disclosure is pretty new; she is so
angry and hurt and in such pain. It is so hard to watch
her because I am watching myself. I am pretty focused
on the fact that I have to sit up and take responsibility
for my behavior and hopefully leave a lot of my bad
behavior behind. I feel ready to go home and take care
of my kids in a better frame of mind. I guess I really
did need to step back and get out of my life in Myrtle
Beach in order to see things more clearly. I have to do
my First Step for COSA (for spouses of sex addicts). It
is really daunting because there are about twenty-five
questions to answer, plus two long lists of inventories
to do. I have to get that done, because then I need to
do the same thing on anger.

...Had a great COSA meeting. Really like the two
women who showed up. It is so sad to see what has
happened to all of our spirits. Somewhere along
our lives, we lost a sense of ourselves and got swept
away. I am through allowing that to happen to my life
anymore. I am through living my live through or for
other people.

...Wow. What a day. I took part in another group's
family week session. I cried when I gave my feedback.
I know I am not supposed to get caught up with other
people's stuff, but I couldn't help it. I hate seeing
someone else's mother cry, and I hate seeing kids cry.

Am all caught up in my homework. I want everything put behind me, so I can really focus on family week. That is really going to be intense.

September 1, 2000

…Today I am a little down. I am really worried about next week. Having to sit in that chair and hear all the shit I have done to the kids is going to be terrible. My goal is not to cry because if I lose it, then the kids won't be comfortable sharing their feelings. So, I have to pray for strength. I realize I can't control what anyone does, and hope we can heal from this. All my close friends are in their family week, so I don't see them much. I am due to be discharged on the sixteenth, but I am leaving on the fourteenth. They really don't do squat on Thursday or Friday of your last week so I am almost out of here. I can't believe how fast this has gone. I have to be grateful for this month of self-discovery, new women friends, and the beautiful scenery.

September 2, 2000

This day was the prettiest day we've had here: dry, cool, and sunny. We hit the "beach" (the pool). We all got a little burnt but it felt good. Only had four lectures today. A lot of us are having a hard time sitting so much. I notice a lot of people make fun of the other patients. I have been pretty good about not doing that. I haven't spoken badly about anyone except "phone girl" who yelled at me for taking too much time on the phone. I actually yelled right back at her; she is such a nut case. I know I don't have to like everyone, but I do have to be respectful.

September 3, 2000

...Big crowd in the TV lounge. Everyone watching South Park except me. I just finished doing my list work for Ben; I had to list the ten things that I wanted to say to each of my family members. For example, I had to list the things that Ben had done that really hurt me. They got here today around 1:10. I was really excited and waited out by the parking lot. They drove up in a little rental car and all the kids tumbled out. Olivia came running up when she saw me, giving me a great big hug, and the rest were really happy to see me. Ben was too. We walked around a bit and showed them everything, and then we sat on the lawn. Olivia, Henry, and Harper went swimming. Ben and I got to talk alone, and we had some good things to say. He told me about his doing a Fourth Step on his resentments toward me, and it helped him to see how he reacts to his high expectations of me. He also had to deal with his unrealistic expectations of me in a sexual way. So that was interesting. He also said we can't raise the kids by one or the other parent; it has to be done together.

September 4, 2000

...Had a good day but it was draining—chock full of meetings and lectures. We had our first family group, and I was really proud of the kids. Henry said we had a crummy relationship, and what he hoped to get out of the week was to be a better son! Of course, I lost it when he said that he thinks he may have something to do with my unhappiness! Olivia went next and said pretty much the same thing, her big brown eyes filling up with tears. Watching them crying and in pain was terrible. Ben was OK. My boundaries are pretty strong with him so nothing he said hurt me. Then I had to tell

the kids about my responsibility, and I cried as I told
them all that I blew them off or yelled at them because
I was angry at their dad and overwhelmed by what
had happened. They had nothing to do with it.

…my therapist was so nice. Even she teared up. She
pulled me aside and gave me a quick hug and told me
there would be a lot less people in rehab if there were
more parents like me who took responsibility for their
behavior and let their children speak their own truths.
That made me feel a little better, but not much.

…Even though the listing will be gut-wrenching
for me to listen to—it will be worth it for me, and
hopefully it will help the kids. I do find it funny that I
am the one in the hot seat and not Ben. The kids and
I never had this opportunity to do family listing and
accountability while he was at Menninger. But this
week is about my behavior, and what this has cost my
family—not about Ben's. Tomorrow is my big day to
talk to Dr. Patrick Carnes.

September 5, 2000

…Just had my meeting with Dr. Carnes. What a full-
circle moment for me to meet him face to face. He
was really wonderful. Very easy to talk to. I told him
about the disclosure and the way it was done over the
phone. He thinks I should sit with Harold and Ben
and he should tell me more details of Ben's behavior,
or, I could do it out here with another therapist of my
choosing. Then, I have to address the rage and anger I
have for Ben. The rage is toxic and I have to let it go or
it will ruin the marriage. He can tell I am still holding
on because of the power I still give the gawking and
the phone call from rehab three years ago. My only
way to have this marriage work is for me to be able

to make peace with this. I asked him if he thought my marriage was doable and he said, "definitely"—If I am willing to follow through on my own recovery. He also said he enjoys Harold so much, and that there are quite a few sex addicts in Myrtle Beach! That was funny. I feel kind of elated and hopeful right now.

...I have finally gotten through a really rough day. I was listed by the kids—one by one—and it was difficult. When they cried, I cried. Plus, everyone in my group and their families were there, so I was ashamed of myself as a mother. But, I withstood it and took responsibility for my stinging words and anger. It actually wasn't as bad as I thought it was going to be. They didn't have very much on their lists at all—a couple of specific instances when I said something hurtful or yelled in a way that scared them. The feedback from my friends in the group was really loving and kind—both to the kids and me. I can't even think of yelling after what I have learned here. Ella is going to list Ben privately—without me there but with my therapist. Ben and I are doing our lists privately tomorrow; the kids cannot know details of his behavior.

September 7, 2000

...Nervous and up early. Went out to watch the sunrise. Yesterday was good. I was listed by Ben first, and it was all about me scolding him or shaming him. It is amazing how much he keeps bottled up inside him. I had no idea I was like that.

...Then I did my thing and I got a lot out there. Sue, the therapist, really came through for me, especially with making Ben see the light about his taking his parent's and friends' sides over mine. He has had it all wrong; the wife needs to come first—period. Parents and friends come next. Finally, someone confronts him about that and puts him on notice about his screwy relationships.

...Ben and I met with Dr. Carnes together! It was really interesting. He thinks our marriage has a shot if we both pursue strong recovery paths.

After our meeting with Dr. Carnes, I dragged Ben in for a joint session with another therapist. He was great. First he went over with me how I had to get a handle on my raging behavior. I think Ben was probably sitting there enjoying seeing me in the hot seat. Then the other therapist turned to Ben and said, "And you, you have to deal with this enmeshment with your mother." It was great. I wanted to jump up and give him a kiss for that!

September 13, 2000

...Today has been good. I graduated from my group, and that was really moving. Everyone said such nice things, and made me feel really upbeat and strong.

...Here I go, my last official meeting with a therapist at the Meadows. I had a great session. I guess I feel comfortable with him because he has a Boston accent and he reminds me of Harold—no bullshit, no letting you off the hook. We went over the general issue of anger with men, as well as how I give men all my power, and how I have been trained to believe that I am less than them, just because I am a female. Then we hit on self-love, taking care of myself first, and not putting all of my energy into Ben. I asked him if maybe we should live separately for a month or two, while I adjust to being home. He said that was a lousy idea, because I would be physically away from him

but not emotionally. I would probably fall back into
the trap of being consumed by what he was doing. So,
I am an addict. I am addicted to my frigging husband.
He said I haven't fully learned the concept of healthy
detachment yet. Bob left me with this: Once I know
and live my life in a self-love mode, then I can find out
for myself if it is right to be with Ben. He said I will
know soon if I follow a self-love program. It was good,
sound advice. He's my favorite therapist out here.

I was learning that the traits of co-addicts are sometimes
difficult to understand. A lot of different words were used to describe
people like me: *enabler, codependent, protector.* I was learning that those
who live with addicts become their protectors, enabling them by
tolerating their addictions.

After all those sessions at the Meadows, Ben and I were filled
with hope and recommitted to each other and our family. We had
finally resolved that we were going to do this and make it work.

On the flight home I did have a fear of going home. I realized
that I flourished without Ben around. I did't need anyone else to define
me. I needed to remember to stop carrying shame that is not mine to
carry. I must believe in my own self-worth. I was afraid I would get
sucked back in to the Ben Syndrome. That's what I began to call my
addiction to him. I thanked God that I had this opportunity to look at
our complicated relationship.

September 18, 2000

…Here I am at the beach house hanging out. I have
had a really nice day. Have been laying low. Slept
until 10 A.M. Ben is very nice. Called me three times
already today and brought home lunch. It has rained
hard all day due to remnants from a tropical storm.
Went to see Harold at 1 P.M. It was good to see him.
There was so much to talk about that the hour flew by.
I will be seeing him twice a week for a while until I
feel comfortable to go to once a week. Yesterday was a

trip. Flying home took all fucking day. Finally landed at 8:30 P.M. Left Scottsdale at 4:30. I had to stop at Chicago Midway. That place is gross. The people creep me out, and everyone is so pale looking and unhappy. I am not used to being out in public.

Once home, I got back into the daily swing of things in Myrtle Beach. I was a new and improved Maurita. I had zero tolerance for Ben's smug attitude when he'd get that way. My goal was to confront him in a nonthreatening way that also let me articulate "my truth," as they say at the Meadows. Someone at the Meadows made the observation that Ben may have three years of sobriety, but his attitudes and perceptions of his world are still so arrogant and puffed up. He comes across as so self-absorbed, and other people see that side of him—not just me.

Ben and I continued in our therapy sessions with Stuart, as a couple. We saw him two or three times a month, for about six months. Shortly after I returned from the Meadows, Ben started to take a downward spiral in his recovery.

September 22, 2000

…Had a pretty good day for myself. Did a little confrontation with Ben about his stupid, arrogant attitude. Harold wants me to bring this up today in our joint session with Stuart. Went to Al-Anon and it was great. It was about rage and anger and, boy, could I relate!

…went to Stuart's with Ben. He was angry and defensive when I started talking about where the hell all of this resentment and disrespectfulness is coming from. I am sick to death of it and won't accept any of it. Stuart said this about our exchange—that Ben went to his little boy mode and I went to my adult/critical parent mode. I personally think I was much more the adult; he said I was much more the critical parent. Whatever. It felt so good to be heard and to stick up for myself. Realizing when he acts like a jerk he is replaying his childhood shit with his mother. Ben is depressed and more distant since our session. It feels good not getting caught up in his feelings—I am doing what I am supposed to be doing.

In the midst of all this therapy, something profound happened. I woke one night to find Ben crying while watching the movie, *Simpatico*. When I asked him if he was all right, he broke down. I had never seen him cry like this.

He said he felt a wave of guilt about the pain he had caused me. He said he was a coward who couldn't face his misdeeds. He said that the ultimate way to prove to me that he understood my pain would be to blow his brains out. I asked him if he had told anyone about these thoughts of self-harm, and he said no. Every time he looked at me, he was reminded of the damage he had done. He called himself a coward again, and he couldn't look my father in the eye because he is so ashamed of himself. Ben believed my father knew about his sex addiction.

I was blown away by this conversation. Of course, killing himself would be the ultimate, selfish act to get back at me. I didn't think he would ever do it, but I have also learned, never say never.

The day before my forty-fourth birthday, I made a gratitude list. My goal for the 44th year was to live the way God intended me to live—free-spirited, kind, and creative. Here is my list.

1. I am grateful for my health.
2. I am grateful for my four beautiful children.
3. I am grateful for a husband who has the guts and courage to look at himself and work on his demons and try hard to recover his wife, his family, and his spirit.
4. I am grateful that I am married to a man who can make a decent, honest living.

5. I am grateful for having all these kooky animals.
6. I am grateful for having this house, not to mention, my beautiful beach house.
7. I am grateful for my birthday present—a CD player for my car.
8. I am grateful for Harold and Stuart.
9. I am grateful for the people who love me even though I don't know it.
10. I am grateful to have hope and knowledge that I can make my own choices.

October 4, 2000

We had bad news about our friend Jenny. They are opting for chemo and radiation instead of removing the cancer. If that is true, she is coming home to die. Her story is just so unbelievable because it has happened so fast. We have no idea why we each are here—and we can drive ourselves crazy trying to figure out the answers that we have no idea about. Why Jenny? I think the question is, do I believe God has sent us here for a specific reason? Or, do life circumstances happen randomly? I don't believe we are here by chance. I have just noticed I now have frown lines on my face. My life is stressing me out and aging me before my time.

October 5, 2000

My birthday.

…Big deal, it's my birthday. Actually it is because I am healthy and alive! Ben got up and made me breakfast and gave me a dozen roses. Nice start. My parents called and they were funny. My father is very alarmed and said he thinks I should stop seeing all these therapists and start having the counsel of a good lawyer waiting in the wings. At least I know they will be OK with a divorce, and that they will embrace the kids and me if I do have to walk away. I am so against divorce, but maybe I am being brainwashed by all this therapy. We are in the hole $70 and we have a whole week to go before pay day. Great.

October 9, 2000

…Last night we both cooked dinner together. I made the bread and noodles, Ben made the sauce. I set the table and made sure everything was cleaned up. We did OK—a normal family dinner!

…Got kicked in the stomach today by someone very new to recovery, who told me that her husband (a doctor who is as sick as they come and not in recovery) heard that Ben had multiple love affairs around town! I wish. What is she possibly thinking by telling me that? Very nice. Ruined my day. Like I need another bad day.

I made a pledge to myself to be an effective partner. I signed my name to a commitment to cook four dinners a week and be in charge of getting the kids off to school each morning. Removing that argument from our lives allowed us to sit and discuss our budget without tearing each other apart. In exchange, Ben signed his name to a statement that he would work around the house on Sunday afternoons. Harold was proud of us for our grownup give and take agreements. He also decided I was strong enough to cut back and see him once a week. It made me a little uneasy, but I knew I was stronger emotionally.

I also focused on my physical health, running on the beach and hitting the gym once in a while. One day, I had lunch with a woman named Donna. Her husband had contacted Ben about a support group for spouses of sex addicts, and Ben set me up with her. There we were, holding Myrtle Beach's first unofficial COSA meeting in a back booth of a local pancake house. We were just two people having breakfast and talking about the impact of sexual addiction on our lives.

She was so heartbroken, and while we hadn't discussed her entire story during that first meeting, I did exactly what I wished someone had done for me at the beginning stages of my recovery. I told her that it was not her fault and that she was not alone. Every couple of minutes during our time together, I felt so excited—finally, another woman has come forward in my own community.

October 11, 2000

...I have to get an official meeting going. I feel stupid reading all the introductions, Steps, etc. when it is just the two of us each week. I know I have to get this damn meeting started. Maybe this is how I give back, although I can't think of anything sicker to have to help women with. I never want anyone to go through something like this alone—ever—like I had to because it SUCKS!

October 23, 2000

Well, where do I start? Friday was a very strange day. We ended up at Stuart's, thanks to an emergency session because of Ben's behavior. He came in about ten minutes late. He was so smug and cruel and sabotaging. Stuart called him on it almost immediately. Ben made the comment like, "It was just sex—no big deal." He actually said that and shrugged his shoulders. I looked at him like he was a complete stranger. What an idiot! He went on to say that the addict in him is trying to kill himself and kill our marriage. At every moment he is at war with himself.

Stuart was very alarmed. Ben is in a black hole and having suicidal ideology. My heart was pounding because Ben was acting so strange—mocking Stuart and me and this whole recovery process. As we left, Ben said he wouldn't be able to be stopped if killing himself was what he was going to do. One minute this guy is one way, and I turn around and he is someone else. I never know what I am walking into. I know I am no angel by any stretch, but his behavior is so much more bizarre.

…Over dinner I expressed my feelings about the fear I felt about his behavior. He is struggling with just about everything. He has relapsed with masturbation again. What a nut case he is.

October 24, 2000

…Ben is still really struggling. Didn't want to get out of bed and face the day. Went to Harold's. He does not believe that Ben is suicidal, but he is going through a tough time and wants to act out. Harold wants me to show Ben empathy and let him know I hear his struggles. At the same time, I can't allow myself to buy into Ben's behavior in a way that negatively affects my behavior.

October 25, 2000

…Had a long day. Am feeling sad. I am all wrapped up in my weird little world. Had a busy day—got the kids breakfast, carpooled, dropped off the dogs at the vet, met with Stuart, cracked up inappropriately at something Stuart said, so I got yelled at. Took Ben to the deli for a bagel. Met Charlie for lunch and that was great. Told him a lot about what was going on and what I had been feeling. He was sweet and nonjudgmental. Then he told me some funny stories about his current relationships and his one slip up in Charleston. It was funny, and I love that he was so honest with me.

After lunch, Charlie took me back to his car and he wanted me to listen to this woman's testimony on tape. She was a sex addict from some church in California. It was very honest—even though she was the betrayer—and it was tough to listen to. Her marriage ended after her disclosure, so I was really disappointed in that. Why didn't Charlie play this for Ben? She is happily remarried—big deal. It was funny because I told Charlie I almost started crying, but I didn't want to cry in front of him. And then he said he almost started crying, but he didn't want to cry in front of me! Then we gave each other a hug and I left.

November 2000

I had a real turning point today. I ran and organized our first COSA meeting! Harold got us a room at Bob Barrow's church down in Pawley's. It was wonderful. We used the COSA meeting guidelines I brought back from the Meadows, plus that great betrayal book that I bought in the bookstore. We have agreed to use that as our book for now. Beth, Donna, and me are the first official members. What a day. Over three years in the making. I have to be careful not to be a Miss Know-it-all and remember not to give advice and pretend I know all the answers. I must remain humble. Donna's questions are gut wrenching. Some issues I haven't dealt with and some I have. All I know is this is going to be an incredible experience. The next thing we are going to do is get a phone number so people can call. After the meeting, I felt really good and grateful. Thank you, God, for this day and my first real COSA meeting in this town. Thank you for my feeling of gratitude.

December 2000

Jenny died this morning. I am kind of glad because her poor body has taken such a beating. I am so sad for the family she has left behind. Tomorrow is her memorial service. I believe it will be packed.

December 30, 2000

This morning was Jenny's memorial service. The church was full. It was a wonderful tribute to Jenny and her family. One of their boys was in the receiving line and he looked so beautiful and sweet. It must be just the hardest thing to say good-bye to your own young children. How does a mother do that? To face that is unimaginable.

January 1, 2001

Happy New Year! Had a ridiculous call from my sister-in-law today. She wanted to know why my in-laws hadn't received our family Christmas card! I said, "I don't know. Why don't you ask your brother?" So she calls Ben back, and he tells her he purposely left his mother off the Christmas card list to get back at her. He also said he uses the same tactic with me. When he feels attacked he will retaliate by isolating and ignoring. This ridiculous, childish conversation was done in front of the kids and me. Ella finally told him to be quiet. I told him to get off the couch and go into the study. What an ass. I honestly thought he sent his parents a card—as he did last year and the year before. He asked me at least twice if I had extras because he wanted to send out five to his family. I sent out eighty, and he just had to send five. Now he is feeling guilty and angry at himself for fucking up and realizing he didn't make any effort toward his own family during the holidays. Had fun at Charlie's party last night. Had a really nice time in spite of Ben.

January 2, 2001

…Went to Al-Anon and it was a good mix of people. Finally have a couple of women there who are my age, so it's nice to have some contemporaries. Of course I love the older women there too; they have been through so much. The topic was freedom.

…went to Harold's and had a good session there as well. I talked about what happened New Year's day and my sister-in-law's ridiculous phone call with Ben. Harold can't believe I put up with his controlling and disrespectful behavior, especially when it is done in front of the kids and aimed at me. He said the healthier I get the more these things are going to become so apparent. Also told H. that I doubted my ability to earn a decent living to support the kids and me. He said he had no doubt that I could do anything I wanted to do; it is my lack of self-discipline and focus that continues to sabotage me. It was a good session and felt upbeat when I left.

…I am doing better with communication, and I am taking more care in reaching out to other women in recovery. Made sure I called my parents and wished them a Happy New Year and told them both that I loved them. My Mom is OK and can say it back but Dad sputters out something like, "Thank you."

….scheduled a breakfast with the doctor's wife who has finally realized what her husband is up to. She has found a bunch of credit card receipts for porn tapes and hotel receipts involving escort services. It is really sad because she has such young children.

January 7, 2001

…Ben is off on an AA retreat with a bunch of guys. He just called to check in. I didn't even ask him to. How ironic that I don't really care anymore if he calls when he is away and now he calls without me asking.

…I am feeling a little stronger and a little freer. I think hanging out with my new COSA friends is forcing me to realize how much I have been through and how much I have come through. I am becoming a better human being to boot! I am continuing to plug away at the house instead of continuing to complain and play miss victim.

January 10, 2001

…four people called me yesterday to go to the introductory women's BSF (Bible Study Fellowship) that is popular in town. It's a conspiracy. I didn't even know one woman. I certainly didn't return anyone's call. Ben and Henry leave for the Bahamas to visit Charlie tomorrow for five days. I am looking forward to the break.

January 22, 2001

…Busy day. The best part of my day was COSA. I met a woman who has a lot of recovery in S-Anon. S-Anon is just like COSA—specific to spouses of sex addicts! She just moved here from New York and she is happy to have found our meeting. She has a lot of meeting material we can use. I can't wait to talk to her again. Beth brought her; they met at an Al-Anon meeting. So this is very exciting. Came home, took a short nap, had a horrible run, and drove the kids all over the place. I think I may even take Tuscon to the beach house Saturday night and all day Sunday.

January 23, 2001

I am scared to death and freaked out. Harold thinks
I am ready to face my life without him in it. I do not
feel ready at all, not with Ben and me still having
such ups and downs. He told me things that make me
feel hopeful that I can do this; the problem is, I don't
want to. Now I have to focus all my attention on my
marriage and making decisions on my own again, and
I don't want to do that. As Stuart says, I am on the cliff
and don't feel ready to jump into the water. Ben is just
still too unsafe and unstable in my eyes.

February 11, 2001, morning

…We are so distant. Ben slept in Henry's room
last night. Was the first time in weeks that I slept
peacefully through the night, so I feel well rested. It
is a beautiful, dry sunny day. I have to get up and get
ready for our day down at that church in Pawleys
Island. Ben has become friendly with the Senior
Pastor, Bob. Ben is going to speak at a recovery lecture
and then we will go out to lunch with Bob and his
wife, Lydia. I haven't met her yet, so this should be
interesting. I have asked God to please help me keep
my mouth shut and not say anything inappropriate
or hurtful. I am, as usual, in turmoil. I still feel, after
all this time, that I don't know what to do with my
marriage.

February 11, 2001, evening

…Had a difficult day today. Ben is distant and
withdrawn. He did a wonderful job talking to a group
of people at the church. He said I was a powerful,
strong woman and that he loved me more than
anything! He has never said that before in such a
public way. Why doesn't he show me that at home?

Lydia, Bob's wife, is a doll. I really liked her and we hit it off. I was a little emotional with her and told her a lot. I cried at lunch because I told her we are at the end. I said the scope of the infidelity was just too much for my heart to heal from. The kids are constantly fighting, the house is falling apart, our finances are all screwed up—it is all just too much. It is obvious talking to Lydia that I am still in a boatload of pain. Would I be like this if I had divorced him when he first came clean?

February 13, 2001

Oh, what a night we had. Last night was horrible. We sat in the study and talked about how bad things are going. Ben started off by apologizing for his remoteness and his withdrawal. Then he just looked so beat up and sad as we sat there and discussed a legal separation. I was sitting in the big leather chair and as the conversation went on, I started crying harder and harder and felt smaller and smaller. I love him, but I hate what he has done. This marriage is empty, and we both know it. I am feeling totally alone. Every dream is dead. I don't know what is going to happen. We are going to spend the night here and then I will drive him to the airport at 1:00 for his ski trip. This is perfect timing and will give us some private time to think about how to go about ending the marriage.

February 27, 2001

...So much has happened since I last wrote anything. The biggest, saddest news is that Jack, a friend of Ben's, died of a drug overdose in Charleston last Wednesday. It was all so sad—I was talking to Cyndi on the phone and at the end of our conversation she asked if I had heard about Jack. He had relapsed and was supposedly checking into a place in Charleston. I told her that Ben had gotten a couple of distress calls from Jack, but he was drugged up so Ben didn't return his calls because he knew he was high. Well, the next day he died—alone—in a hotel room. Just so sad and a waste. He was such a kind-hearted guy and he just couldn't find any peace. The funeral was Sunday.

...I am really broken hearted. Today is Wednesday and it is Stuart day. I got up and walked out of the session. I don't think we can take this anymore. Ben opened up that he is totally miserable and on the edge. He is really hurting about Jack, as they were great friends. He said if it weren't for what happens to the people left behind when you kill yourself—he would do it in a heartbeat. Nice. Marriage is in a horrible place. His business is in serious trouble. Has a severe cash shortage. So Stuart tries to get us to do some silly handholding exercise and I just couldn't do it anymore. I just walked out. Let's get a divorce.

...Ben and Henry just left for the beach house for the night. We are both pussyfooting around the divorce issue, but separating is an open topic.

March 2001

...I am really suffering. Am caught between separating or not. Went to S-Anon and cried a little as did Barbara. I am so lucky to have Beth and Barbara in my life. I admire them so much. And they were really there for me today.

March 2001

Wow, how time flies. There are times when I want to sit and write and times when I couldn't be bothered. I am here at the beach house with Roxie. I got a free

night out because I beat Ben at miniature golf. I am
in a pretty upbeat frame of mind. I credit that to
more praying in the morning and being vigorous in
attending my meetings. Even started making a better
effort go to Al-Anon again. Finally talked to Harold
for a one-time meeting and it was good. I filled him in
on everything I was feeling. He heard me out and was
really helpful.

….My relationship with Ben is better. We are having a
little more fun together. Unfortunately, he has taken a
real downturn with his depression. He is commenting
about women, skipping meetings, isolating, and not
returning phone calls from the other sex nuts. I try not
to react because that is what he is looking for—my
reaction.

We are very concerned about Ella. She broke down
and admitted she is failing two classes! This from
a child who has never given us any problems with
grades. She has always been an excellent student;
her obsession with her appearance is taking all her
energy and time. Her emotional upheaval is now
controlling her. We have to take some action with her
immediately.

My assignment from my therapist Stuart this week is
to "free-associate the word *humiliation*." What a nut.

Chapter Twelve. Never Say Never

ഔരു

There was a horrible darkness looming larger by the day, creeping its way into my life, and it had nothing to do with my husband. It was, instead, my father.

May 16, 2001

I'm at the beach house. I haven't felt like writing much. I think I am getting bored with writing the same old thing all the time. Two good days, one bad or vice versa. The big news is that my Dad has a new potentially life-threatening health problem. His bone marrow has stopped producing blood cells so he is very weak. He will have to have blood transfusions periodically. All we can do for the moment is wait and see. I had to force my mother to go back to Vermont two weeks early. She didn't want to leave and be with my father! We packed up all her stuff for her and I think one of my brothers-in-law will fly down here and drive her car back to Vermont for her.

May 19, 2001

Had a nice day today. Ben is up at Harold's retreat. The eminent financial meltdown has begun. Ben's quitter attitude really makes me sick. The mean, unspiritual side of me wants to tell him what I really think of him but all it would do is hurt his feelings. As I sat on the beach today, my heart just gets sick thinking about having to sell this beach house. I am angry at God for all of this.

May 29, 2001

The decision is clear. To get out of the financial drain of the mortgage on Ben's office building, we have to sell my beloved beach house. It is the only thing we have left in our life that is good, and now that even has to go. God hates me. I am trying to spend as much time here as possible. Mentioned this to a friend of mine and she gave me the name of a good lawyer. Divorce or beach house? Keep family together and be financially responsible for our debt or fuck everything and take the beach house in a divorce settlement? I hate having to do the right thing.

...I decided to get Olivia and Harper dinner at the Garden City McDonald's. Harper was in the passenger side. As I crossed the cut-in lane, I got nailed by a red Yukon that was speeding in the turn-off lane. We got hit but we spun around and were unhurt, by the grace of God. One second slower on my part and Harper would have been crushed. I was really shaken up and just wanted to sit for a second and cry—out of shock and relief. The whole rear bumper was ripped off and a taillight was smashed. I remained calm with Harper and told her to get out of the car and go get dinner while I called Ben and the police. Ben came and was very angry that I crashed his car and was the one cited for the accident—my first one in thirty years! I didn't think I was the one at fault. Never mind that we could have been killed. As usual, my husband showed no emotional support; all he cared about was his fucking car. Went back to the beach and just sat there. I want out. Period. I don't even like him anymore as a human being.

...Went to S-Anon this morning and went to breakfast with everyone. Pulled out of my pity as Donna is dealing with much worse stuff than me.

June 17, 2001

The big news to report and what I have been putting off seeing in print is that my father is dying. I can't believe his time has come. I really dread the months ahead. From what Ben understands it could be a matter of months or weeks depending on how his body reacts to his treatments and where his mind is in dealing with this news. He hasn't been doing well since he left Myrtle Beach in May. We found out last Wednesday that they think he has liver cancer, a small cancer on his colon, and big time problems producing red blood cells. Tomorrow he is going to a specialist at Dartmouth and we will have a better grip about where he stands.

Ella's first appointment with the obsessive compulsive disorder (OCD) specialist in Charleston went better than we could have hoped. With a proper course of medication for the OCD and cognitive behaviorial therapy, she should live a fairly normal life. There is a group in Mt. Pleasant that will be a good fit for her, and I think she is relieved that it isn't a complicated diagnosis.

Ben's mood still swings as uneven as his golf game. The only difference lately is whether or not I give his fire fuel to grow or squash it by ignoring it. I'm getting better at diffusing his need for attention by not giving him any. I don't have the time lately to wallow in my own selfish crap or to give undue attention to Ben as he acts out and looks for attention.

Henry and I jumped on a flight north to Boston to help out my parents and see my Dad. We upgraded our rental car to a Jeep for the drive from Boston to Vermont, and I let Henry listen to his own CDs on the way. We drove through Woodstock on the way there. It's one of my favorite towns. We had some good talks about his Dad and his Grandpa. Henry is such a good kid.

July 14, 2001. Vermont

What a melancholy, sad time this is. My Dad is weaker by the day and not showing any signs of improvement. He has gotten worse since Henry and I got here. Every morning I have gotten up and made him breakfast, and this morning right before he sat down to eat he threw up all the Milk of Magnesia. It was horrible because my mother flipped out and yelled, "I have to get to my water aerobics class." Then she walked out the door, right past the vomit and everything. Henry helped me clean things up. My poor Dad is angry and frustrated that his body is failing him. The first time he saw me this visit, he was lying on the bed in the upstairs bedroom and he started crying. I laid down next to him trying my hardest not to break down. I asked him if he was afraid to die, and he said, "No." He believed in everlasting life and in God so he wasn't afraid. I am able to shrug off his grumpiness and short temper because I know he doesn't mean it. Thank goodness for recovery principles. My mother vacillates between being kind and loving to being angry and reactive. She gets very defensive and scared, so I am trying not to be judgmental about her behavior. She is watching her husband die a horrible death. She told me yesterday that Dad's hematologist is not optimistic about Dad's prognosis. She asked me if I would stay on and go with them on the 20th. I really need to get home for a few days to take Henry back and get Olivia's birthday plans rolling, so I am going to come back on the 19th with Ben. Dad threw a fit and said he didn't want anyone to go with them, but I said Mother asked me to. Then he said fine but he didn't

want Ben to come here to "put his two cents in" and I
said he would never butt in. I now know he hates Ben
and is disgusted with him because thanks to my big-
mouthed sister—my whole extended family knows
about his sex addiction.

I have teared up a couple of times watching my Dad go
through this horrible time but I don't want to lose it in front of my
parents. On the Henry front we have had a pretty good time. He is so
easy and is amusing himself with the computer and helping my Dad
do some stuff on line.

My sister Lindsay was having a tough time of it. Dad was just
feeling so sick and my Mom's mood swings were hard on Lindsay.
Still, I felt my mother needed to get a grip on her temper. My father
deserves a quiet and peaceful environment to deal with his illness. To
my mother's credit, she took my advice and got herself a therapist.
I think she realized that she needed some help to handle things
differently during my father's dying process.

July 21, 2001

I am back in Vermont, this time with Ben. I have been
wrapped up in my own world. Lost in thought about
my sadness and dread about losing my Dad.

Lindsay and my mother still struggled with being around each
other. Lindsay was a wounded soul in need of compassion, patience,
and love from my mother. Yet my mother, who was dealing with the
reality of losing a man she had shared her life with for more that fifty
years, was unable to share much of herself. In watching my mother
and Lindsay's interaction, I realized that Lindsay, like me, struggled
in similar ways. After all, we were brought up in the same family. My
own struggles have probably had a big impact on my own children,
and that might be part of the reason why Ella is starting her OCD
therapy next week. Family dysfunction cycles through generations,
and it takes strength, conviction, and the willingness to see through a
lot of bullshit to end those patterns.

With everything going on in my life, I had turned to survival mode which didn't leave me a lot of time to think about my anger or marriage troubles. Otherwise, I would have said something demoralizing to Ben about our finances when I had to plunder the stocks just to pay monthly bills again.

August 1, 2001. Hampton Inn, Myrtle Beach

…. Am spending the day and night with Olivia to make up for missing her birthday last week.

My brother David came up to Vermont on the day that I was leaving my parents' house. By this time, my siblings had all decided we would take turns and rotate our time with my Dad so that my parents were not alone. Apparently, my father's first words to David were along the lines of, it was "a disgrace for a fine institution like PBS to ever show his documentary on HIV." David turned around and left the hospital room. He said he walked around for about an hour to calm himself down and then went back into his room. My Dad apologized to my brother, saying that he was sorry, but that was how he felt. That was so sad for me to hear.

I had been keeping to myself as I went through the emotions of the past couple of weeks. The imminent death of my father, the behavior of my Mom and siblings, and other family dysfunction had prompted me to call Harold.

"And that's fine, Mo," Harold told me during our once-in-a-while sessions. "Understanding that you need help is a sign of strong and capable emotional people. It's that denial of help, that arrogant attitude of 'I can handle all of this' that is dangerous."

Harold was really helpful in allowing me room to breathe as I dealt with family issues. Because of my years of therapy, I had developed a no-bullshit filter in my life. I knew that my Dad was dying in a few weeks and my time was best spent making him comfortable and keeping my sadness out of the way of his peace and tranquility.

August 11, 2001

...Wow, I am off to Vermont tomorrow with Olivia. My family dynamics are now really crazy. Everyone of us is reacting to this crisis so differently. Lindsay is helping out in a big way but doesn't have any outlet for her obvious pain. Everyday that I speak to her, she breaks down, probably out of fear and sadness.

...I have said all I want to say to my Dad at this moment, so now feel a need to just sit with him—be a fresh, loving face in the house. My mother sounded so broken and sad. I am torn because I don't want to go. I heard the relief in my mother's voice when David said I was going to be there.

August 24, 2001

...Have had a really tough time lately. Have a little bit of a hangover thanks to three glasses of wine last night. Smart. Harold warned me not to drink anything during this crisis. I am beginning to buckle under the financial stress we face. We're headed into the toilet, and that is what I get for taking no financial responsibility for myself.

...My poor Mom and Dad are suffering so much in Vermont. I have my own anger, disappointment, and sadness about my life. I am at a standstill and frustrated with my furniture painting. I believe I have the talent and know how, but I am totally frustrated on how to market my work and make a living from it. I don't want something grandiose—just enough to support my children and me.

September 5, 2001

We are flat broke—I mean no money anywhere. I feel
helpless. Ben is paralyzed with making any decisions,
so he chokes and we go deeper in debt. That office
building is an albatross around his neck. Tomorrow
is another humiliating day—I have to plunder our
stock portfolio to pay bills—I hate doing that, it is so
embarrassing. Thanks to all this therapy and rehab, we
have plowed our way through all of our money. Hey,
at least we had the money to plow through, right? Joy.

I woke up early on September 11th, got the kids off to school,
and went back to bed to watch *TODAY*. I was on the phone with Ben
when the first plane hit the Twin Towers.

"Oh, my God, honey, a plane just hit the World Trade Center."

He hung up the phone and went to watch the coverage in his
waiting room, and I continued watching the *TODAY* show. Then the
second plane hit. That was no accident. Crazy people had just flown
planes into the towers. I immediately thought of my brother David.
He lived in SoHo right on Mercer Street and usually jogged a route
every morning around the World Trade Center. My mother called
soon after, letting me know that David and Mike were safe, so that
was a huge relief.

My thoughts went to my kids and what was happening at
their schools. I wondered if they understood or were told what was
going on. It was a horrifying time.

September 19, 2001. Vermont

…Went down the hill to get some bagels and the
morning paper for my Dad. We sat across from each
other reading the *Boston Globe*. There was a page full
of photographs of all the firemen and policemen that
were lost at the trade center. I couldn't help noticing
how young the men were, and that so many were
Irish. I asked him if he ever thought he would see

something like 9/11 in his lifetime and he dropped the
paper down from in front of his face, looked at me,
and said, "No." I noticed he had some jelly on the side
of his lip. I said, "Dad, you have jelly on your lip."
He looked right back at me and said "What do I care?
I'm terminal," and he went right back to reading the
newspaper. I looked back at him with a slight smile,
shaking my head. He was right; he obviously had a lot
more going on in his mind than having to worry about
the impact of 9/11 or jelly on his lip.

September 20, 2001

…Last night my mom went to bed early and I had to
help my Dad get ready for bed. So, I saw everything.
He said, "Unfortunately, you will have to see my
private parts." I tried to make light of it by saying,
"Well, you saw mine when I was little, so now we
will be equal." We kind of smirked at each other at
the absurdity of my comment and the gravity of the
situation. I saw my father naked and his poor body is
just being punished. He looks sometimes like a little
boy. Sometimes I see fear in his eyes and sometimes I
see joy! When I got him settled in his leather recliner
and lit a blazing fire for him, he couldn't have been
more content. He looked over at me and said he would
be happy to die just like that.

I just hope things go well today. I am a little nervous
with Mom leaving and going to the Cape this
weekend. I can't believe she wants to leave him when
Dad is this sick, but I guess she needs a break from
reality. I know I can handle this with God's help. I just
hope nothing traumatic happens on my watch.

September 21, 2001

…Dad and I met with his doctors this morning and the news is devastating. He is getting worse and the transfusions aren't working. His liver is starting to fail, which will lead to other major organs failing. I made sure the doctors clarified all the major points, and I wept a little as they spoke. Dad will not get better and his body is deteriorating. He looked so defeated as he slumped a bit in his wheelchair. He asked his doctor how much time he had if he stopped the transfusions. He had a couple of weeks, at best. We were very clear on what was going on. I brought him home, got him comfortable, and we spent the afternoon together. I had to make two more trips to the emergency room with him during the next twenty-four hours because his clotting is worse…. Lindsay, who has been a great help, and I spent the rest of the day trying to get the catheter to work the way it is supposed to. He is so vulnerable and sweet. All I want is for him to be safe and well-cared for.

September 23, 2001

…Today was a beautiful day in Vermont. It was an emotional one because we talked about Dad having no options left. He wept a couple of times, as I have. I opened the door for us to talk and have everything be out in the open. I asked him stuff like what kind of mass he wanted, or any favorite scripture readings or songs he wanted at his funeral. He said he just wanted a traditional Catholic funeral and told me to pick out the readings. He doesn't have a real favorite. I asked him what he thought his greatest achievement in life was and he said, without missing a beat, "marrying your mother." My mother came home from the Cape today and we sat down and filled her in on what had

176

happened while she was gone. I had a huge knot in my stomach because I couldn't believe I was telling her that her own husband is at the end of his life. Dad took over the conversation and told her that decisions had to be made. I think she was in shock. I felt so sorry for her. It is absolutely unreal what these last few days have been like. He has shown so much courage and humbleness. The other day, he shook hands with all the nurses as he left the transfusion suite for the last time. Some of the nurses hugged him good-bye and wept. He has been through so much and never complains. His mind is so clear, yet his body is dying. What a real test of courage. I love him dearly.

…I just called the kids and am looking forward to going home tomorrow but I am so torn about leaving. I am planning on coming back in two weeks.

October 4, 2001

…Had a difficult day. My mom and Lindsay called today and Lindsay was crying. Apparently, Dad has had enough. Hospice will be stepping in tonight and all other methods of treatment will stop. I will try to get a reservation earlier than the end of the week.

October 5, 2001

Happy Birthday! What a day. First thing this morning Lindsay and my mother called to wish me a happy birthday. Lindsay is crying and believing that he is going to die today—on my birthday, because we have such a strong connection. Boy, I hope he doesn't die today! Spoke to David—he is doing OK. Things are relatively calm. My father is comfortable. Doesn't speak but they believe he can hear what people are saying. I think I have decided to stay put. He is surrounded by enough people and is in good hands.

I would never forgive myself if I was traveling and
got stuck in a plane or airport when he died. To
realize he won't be around anymore is mind-boggling.
Ben went out of his way to do stuff with me and is
being really nice.

October 6, 2001

…Well, my day has come. My father died today. I
can't believe I just wrote that. I was watching TV
on the couch with Ben when my mother called. She
was pretty calm, and then everyone else got on the
phone. He went very peacefully and was surrounded
by his family. He went quickly. As soon as he let go
and gave himself permission to stop treatment, he
was gone in two days. I am grateful he didn't die
yesterday on my birthday. That would have sucked. I
think he died today to spare me that and to have my
older sister make it up there to see him. Who knows?
I am heartbroken.

The funeral was beautiful. The church, St. Paul's in downtown
Wellesley, is old and elegant. My parents were married in that church,
and all of us kids were baptized there. We were amazed at the turnout.
The church was packed. The priest said it was one of the largest
funerals he had ever seen. The great turnout of people made us feel a
little better that day, because we saw what kind of man he had been
and what he meant to so many people. I will be forever grateful that
he was my father here on earth. Then we had a fun yet sad reception
at the Wellesley Country Club, where I was reunited with so many
people from my childhood and high school years, including, my three
best childhood friends, Nancy, Pam, and Debbie. The four of us had
not been altogether in the same room since the fifth grade, so that
was really special. The reception was a fitting good-by for my dad,
as he spent so many happy years there with his good friends and his
beloved game of golf.

After my father died, I went back for a few sessions with
Stuart. I was in agony over something. Even though I believed my
father was in heaven now, I had a tremendous feeling of shame. "Now,
he knows everything," I told Stuart. "He knows that Ben was a huge
cheat, and my dad is going to be so disappointed in me for putting up
with all this."

Stuart looked at me, aghast. He shook his head and said,
"Are you kidding me? Your father is no longer of this Earth. He is not
burdened with petty human feelings like judging you or Ben for what
has happened. I believe that he is looking down on you with absolute
love and admiration, amazed at your courage and proud of how you
have handled yourself."

I felt like a huge weight had been lifted off my shoulders after
that session. I had never said anything about sex addiction or told my
father that Ben had cheated on me. I was always too ashamed to admit
that to him. Stuart's words gave me a huge sense of peace and even
some closure with my relationship with my father. I think about this
session as one of the most decisive, defining, and healing sessions in
the process of my recovery.

My marital stress continued during my grieving process. Ben
was running five or six miles at a time. Without the running he said
that he would walk out on me and the kids, forget sobriety, and go
back to sexual acting out. What a crock of shit. He was feeling sorry for
himself and I refused to get sucked into that.

I was involved in a wonderful weekly Bible study group led by
Lydia Barrows down at All Saints Church in Pawleys Island. This was
my first time being committed to a small group Bible study and the
women in the group were wonderful and kind. Lydia taught the Bible
in a way that a beginner like me could understand and identify with.
This group was a tremendous support for me during the aftermath of
my father's death, not to mention the on-going struggles with Ben's
sexual addiction.

May 13, 2002

…Had a big night over at the beach house. Ben never
was able to settle down, and he had one of the worst

nights he has had since being in recovery. Around 10 P.M. I went to bed to read. Ben was still up watching TV and doing paperwork. He comes to bed late but can't get settled and jumps out of bed saying he has to go for a walk. I let him go, thinking, *All right, here it is, the relapse; he's off to find a prostitute.* But I didn't say anything to him about that.

Thankfully, I was in a fairly calm place. I know I can't control his behavior. He came back fifteen minutes later. He said he went across the street and sat there and cried. Then he came back because he didn't want me to be worried. He tried watching TV again but the cable went out.

That night I had a dream that Ben killed himself by jumping over a balcony. I really do sometimes believe that he will not live to see fifty. He even said so himself.

Charlie and Gail had both been gently prodding me for quite some time to share my story in a church setting—specifically at a church that worked the Celebrate Recovery program. I balked at this when Charlie first asked me to speak. I told him in no uncertain terms that I would not speak out publicly about this. Thanks, but no thanks. "I do not want to be the poster wife for sexual addiction," is what I would say to him.

After giving their request serious thought and realizing that even though my marriage isn't in great shape, I do have a story that would be helpful for other women to hear. I was too much of a chicken to speak in front of my own community, so I told Charlie I would do it out of town. He got together with one of the pastors of our church, Greg Anderson, and they found a church in North Carolina that happened to be getting ready to kick off their first Celebrate Recovery program. They would love for Ben and me to come and give our testimonies at their Sunday service. *Great,* I thought half-heartedly.

July 25, 2002

…Olivia's birthday! Am really struggling. I am giving my testimony for the first time at a small church and I am really up in arms about this. I am feeling like a lamb to slaughter. I am afraid I am going to embarrass myself by crying.

July 29, 2002

…Well, I finally did it. It was really tough. Drove up on a hot, sweltering Saturday. Had dinner at Carabbas with Charlie, Julia, Greg, Joannie, Ben, the Pastor, and his wife. They were very nice and supportive. Got back to the hotel late. Didn't sleep very well because of my nerves.

…Got up and went to the church. It is really at the beginning stages, so it is small and inviting with maybe fifty people, tops. I couldn't believe it, but Gail came all the way from Myrtle Beach this morning just to see me do this with her own eyes! Anyway, Ben went first and he always speaks well in public. He has given his testimony before and had revised it and really acknowledges the pain and anguish he has caused me. He praised my strength. Then I got up, and I got very emotional at first. I had to take a couple of deep breaths and just plowed ahead crying a little at the very beginning. After a minute or two I felt better and was able to do OK. A lot of the women cried. One was really overwhelmed and couldn't even speak to me; she just sobbed and walked away. I know I touched a nerve with some of the men too. The women who came up to speak to me after were so kind. One told me I was her hero. One or two told me I should write a book. So it was definitely worth it. I think I got emotional for two reasons: one , I was caught off guard and really moved by what Ben said; second, I felt so humbled thinking about my new relationship with God and Jesus Christ, knowing how broken I was five years ago, and seeing how much healing has taken place today. It was also the first time I publicly proclaimed my faith. Then we had a nice lunch.

In September of 2002, my mother celebrated her wedding anniversary by herself. I still had to stop myself and remember that my father was gone. In some ways, I still had a deep-set belief that my dad would always be there for me. On his wedding anniversary, I normally could have called him up, told him a few jokes, and congratulated him on making it this long. When I called her to check on her, she seemed sad and resigned about this day, but she didn't show much outward emotion. Thinking back about this year, I honestly can't remember seeing her cry. I, however, let the tears flow freely as thoughts of my father came and went.

October 18, 2002

...I spoke at Celebrate Recovery last night. I was very nervous. It was great that Ronnie and Gail came and that she introduced me. She said such wonderful, loving things about me. Then I began. I think I did all right but I lost it for a minute or two when I talked about forgiveness. I guess saying it publicly and knowing what a fucking battle it was really got to me. The response was great afterwards. Was introduced to so many broken women. I met a woman who wished she had heard me speak nineteen years ago because I probably would have saved her from becoming a sex addict after she divorced her sex addict husband. She

thought there was something wrong with her, so after
her divorce, she set out to prove that theory wrong.
I am humbled by where I am today. I also know that
I will take the time, always, to talk or give whatever
hope or comfort that I can for anyone else caught up in
this hell.

Our nineteenth wedding anniversary was in 2002. I decided to
forget the first fourteen and celebrate the last five. There was an antler
candelabra I'd had my eye on for some time, so I bought it to mark the
occasion. I was excited to surprise Ben by even wanting to celebrate
our anniversary. This marked the first year that I took any initiative to
acknowledge our wedding day. When he saw the new candelabra he
said it was strong and chaotic looking, like our lives.

Five years. It was an important benchmark in the recovery
world. We were odds-on underdogs at the very beginning. We had a 95
percent chance of relapse and a 98 percent chance of divorce in the first
five years. But there we were, in our house watching movies with a set
of chaotic antlers above the fireplace, symbolizing five strong, tough
years. We were beating the odds, and while sometimes the odds were
beating us back, it felt good to at least make it across that threshold.

I didn't find out until March of the next year that we had
just barely crossed the finish line together. Ben called me and asked
me to go to a session with Harold. I agreed, just like every other time
we'd met at Harold's office. It had not occurred to me that it would
be a huge deal. Once in Harold's office, however, Ben had something
unthinkable and crushing to tell me. He explained that one day during
one of Henry's soccer trips to Florida, he had relapsed. He had called
an escort service while the boys were out to dinner with the other
parents. He met up with the escort and made it back to the hotel room
before anyone was the wiser.

There was a distinct difference between this disclosure and his
first disclosure. Ben was not on the phone this time; instead, he was
telling me face to face, reading from a letter. He sat in front of me and
told me what had happened. He had already discussed the episode
with Harold at great length, he had put our pastor Ronnie and his

wife Gail on alert, and Harold made him take an HIV test and bring the written results for me to read. The following entry reveals how the disclosure unfolded.

March 30, 2003

Well, I haven't had a chance to write because of what happened last Friday. Thursday night, Ben said he wanted me to go with him to meet with Harold. At first I said, "No way. I am done with therapy, so no more." But he kept insisting, so by Friday morning I reluctantly agree. Harold even called me on my cell phone to make sure I would be there. I thought Ben had done something illegal or crazy with our finances.

We drove in one car, we sat down, and Harold and I kidded around for a few minutes. Then Harold gently steered us back to why we where there. He said that Ben had some things he wanted to tell me and that some of it was going to be difficult to hear. My heart started pounding. Ben took out a couple of pieces of paper from his pocket and started to read it to me. This was a fucking disclosure!

It turned out he went into relapse mode last summer after losing weight, getting back into exercising, then masturbating. Finally, he got the opportunity to act out on an innocent soccer trip with our son. I sat there stunned, looking back and forth at Ben and Harold's faces. It was shocking. I felt myself drowning all over again. Ben then produced a negative AIDS test. He wore a fucking condom. Thanks, asshole.

Harold was wonderful. He told me he would see me Saturday or Sunday, if need be.

I walked out of the office in total shock. This past week has been horrible. I am so empty and at a loss of what

I am going to do. Divorce, definitely. Where is God in all this? I can't stand Ben to look at me, much less touch me. This marriage is so horribly abusive.

April 1, 2003

Everything is pretty heavy duty. I am trying to be civil. I am really, really depressed. I do not feel like having anything to do with anyone. I am totally confused and disjointed by this life and don't know what I am doing. Went to Harold on Monday and was really depressed and felt like a loser. It is nice having him on my side again. Called Gail first thing and just broke down. I yelled into the phone, "He relapsed" and broke down. We will meet this week. Called Charlie. He sounded sad, for both of us. I am meeting with Gail on Thursday. I feel really funny about my mother being here and not letting her in on what has happened in my life. Too humiliating. I am a freak—again.

April, 2003

This has been one of the worst weeks of my life. I have been really down and very depressed. I can't seem to get out of it. I blew off my meeting and Bible study. My mind is spinning. I had lunch with Gail at Tripp's yesterday, and it was very difficult. I told her the real details of the relapse, and it is so hard to say it out loud, because saying it to someone face-to-face makes it real and so painful and hurtful. I know it sounds so dark and sick to someone who is not dealing with a deeply disturbed husband.

The one thing I know I have to work on is trusting and putting my faith wholly and completely in God and his will and love for me. If I get that, then nothing can bring me down. Gail also pointed out that I must love God conditionally. I need to stop projecting my human limitations, ideas, and my will on Him. Now I am totally confused. She also challenged me and asked me to write down one thing a day that Ben does that is nice or positive! Is she fucking kidding? OK, Gail.

April 6, 2003

Something positive: Ben planted pots and cleaned up the driveway.

April 7, 2003

Positive: He was funny, once.

April 8, 2003

Positive: Ben got up and went to work.

April 9, 2003

Lately I have noticed that he comes home agitated and angry from his Monday night SA meetings. He walked in the door and started yelling at Harper and Olivia over something really trivial, and was angry and rude to me. I cut him off and wouldn't engage in his cesspool of a mind. By the time we sat down to dinner he was miserable. He is at war with himself and doesn't know if he can go on. Good, then don't go on.

April 11, 2003

Another really low, low day. Yesterday we went back and forth with bids and bullshit shenanigans with realtors and the guy buying our beach house. Word is out that we are fucked financially so we are, of course, being low-balled. Ben calls me with the latest offer—he doesn't have the fucking balls to say "yes" to the offer so he makes me say it—otherwise this torture will go on all day. So, I told him to go fuck himself and take the offer. Then I hung up on him. Such a horrible day.

April 13, 2003

I fear God has overestimated how much I can overcome. We did meet with Ronnie today and I think that will really help. Ronnie and Gail are the end of the line for me. If this counseling doesn't work, then I give up. Ronnie, of course, went over the Biblical principles about divorce and why, in God's eyes, I can certainly choose to walk away because of the adultery. But for every one reason I can give him to end the marriage, he said he can give me a thousand on why I should stay! He makes me dizzy.

Can't find one thing the liar did that was positive. Oh, yes, he got up and got in his smelly car and drove to work.

April 14, 2003

I cried in front of my mother when I told her we had sold the beach house. She was very kind but got really uncomfortable when I cried and showed emotion. She made a hasty exit.

I am glad that my sister is coming for the week. I just don't know if I can deal with her comments when I tell her about the relapse. Losing the beach house has been horrible. Another really tough, in-my-face loss. The death of yet another dream. I am running out of things that really matter to me. I only have four left: Ella, Henry, Harper, and Olivia. I know that is a lot—four healthy children.

April 15, 2003

I am really struggling. I go between depression and
fear versus being OK. Harold wanted me to tell Lydia
the whole truth about Ben's relapse. So, I told her
everything. So horrible and painful to say it out loud. I
am totally humiliated.

We were catapulted backward into heavy-duty recovery work
once again. I wanted so badly to get divorced, thinking that God was
telling me Ben would never return to His grace, would never find
again what it was to be a wholesome and loving man. I argued up and
down with Ronnie and Gail about it.

"Maurita, God didn't allow you and Ben to have the strength
to put your lives back together after five years of hard work, only to
have it ripped apart by this one relapse."

"He'll never be better. He'll never stop," I said.

April 17, 2003

Another horrible, depressing, confusing week. My
mother now knows about the relapse. My sister told
my mother more than she needed to know, so now
my mother is afraid for my life. She keeps thinking of
the doctor in Wellesley who murdered his wife in the
woods around Morse's Pond. The wife was getting
ready to divorce him because of his sex addiction to
strip clubs and prostitutes. One of my friends sent
me the article from *People* magazine. This successful
physician was living a double life. He was a family
man, loving husband, and talented physician by
day, but he was a sex addict by night. His wife had
discovered the truth and was in the final stages of
filing for divorce and exposing the truth about their
marriage. He took her for a walk around Morse's Pond
and beat her to death with a blunt object.

I went to Ronnie and Gail's, and it was a very difficult, painful hour. Sat in Ronnie's office and Ben came clean about his sexual behavior, per Harold's encouragement. It was mind-numbing for me. Because Ben gave explicit details. I cried a bit at one point. I felt so low and without hope. Ronnie and Gail were wonderful about it.

There was one good thing today. Ben made the beach house bed up without asking. We are staying in it as much as possible until the closing. Ronnie gave us a couple of assignments: Read the new John Ortberg book, and spend some time together as a couple. And, we have to pray together every day. Joy.

April 24, 2003

I am confused about my relationship with God. I really don't know where I stand in my faith. The crushing blow of losing the beach house makes me feel unloved by Him. I have a terrible sense of doom that nothing will go right in my life again. Not to mention Ben's recent relapse.

Ben and I are civil. No sex continues until his six-month HIV test comes back clean. I don't want to touch him anyway, so who cares?

June 10, 2003

I still can't let Ben touch me. I am truly grossed out by his behavior and can't imagine ever having sex with him again. Ever. I hate people. I don't want to be close to anyone. The pain and emptiness I have felt living with a man who is so deeply troubled has sucked the life out of me.

June 27, 2003

You wouldn't believe it where I am! I am at a retreat run by Harold. Here I sit in the third cabin. My seventh retreat. I am nervous because I know I will have to talk about the details of the relapse.

June 28, 2003

The women here with me are wonderful, except one woman is a dud and so hurt and sick. She is not in a place yet where she can or will look at her own behavior.

We all took turns working on very painful issues. I did OK. Actually, I did more than OK. I have learned to go for broke although I really struggle with it. What am I here for if I don't tell the truth and unburden myself? So, with Harold's help, I did it. He even came over and put his arm around me as I sobbed and told four women—two of whom I had just met—the whole truth about Ben. It was very freeing. Once I said it, it didn't matter so much anymore. I didn't care if anyone in the group was horrified or grossed out. All that mattered was I had at least one person on my side, Harold, in this case. Then he hit on my fantasy/daydreaming/escape thing, which I have never really talked about that much outside of his office and at the Meadows. I have been doing this since I was a child—daydreaming about being in another family. It has been a huge piece of my life and so commonplace that I never knew how dysfunctional it has been until recently. For me, it is like a drug. So, it was definitely a growing experience.

July 2, 2003

I am tired and hot and my new testimony is looming ahead. I finally got my testimony ready and made it down to Valerie's church just in time. I was really touched because a couple of my women friends in recovery were there to cheer me on.

A sweet girl told me afterward that her husband is out doing the same things. She cried as she talked about her suffering. I broke down a bit when I spoke about the relapse. I even heard people gasp. I knew I would break down, but I realize I have to continually get things out of my system. Here is my new motto: *Pain, Truth, Heal. Pain, Truth, Heal.*

August 21, 2003

For Ben's forty-eighth birthday, I surprised him and rented a hotel room for the night. I had a massage scheduled for him. That was great; I think he really appreciated it. The kids came to the hotel and met us for dinner. Ella got some balloons and hats and decorated the table, so it was a really good family night.

Right now Ben and I are getting along all right. One day at a time.

October 4, 2003

Has been too long since I have journaled, but this should change because I am part of an unbelievable group going through the Twelve Steps of Celebrate Recovery. I have been complaining to Harold about the lack of healthy role models in recovery for me and told him what a great group it would be if we could get Joannie, Gail, and Lydia all in the same group. But who would lead us? Well, I don't know how he did it. Lynn is chairing the group. I adore all these women so I am really excited. What a group—I can't wait to start.

Ben and I are getting along pretty well. We have turned
the corner after dealing with some real serious shit.

November 8, 2003

My Purpose Driven Life group has started. I don't
know about this. We watch a video for fifteen minutes
and then sit around and talk about it. I feel a little let
down about all the hoopla surrounding this book. I
thought if you really paid attention you would find
your purpose and what you are supposed to be doing
with your career. It is actually five principles of God's
purpose for your life. Everyone has the same purpose.
I think that is so lame.

My other group at Lynn's is really incredible. I have
cried almost every time. I don't know why. Lynn is a
good leader and in control. She is very honest and is
going through a huge change in her own life.

The big news is, I have decided to get baptized in a
pool at the church. Gail challenged me to do it, so after
thinking about it a bit and getting really interesting
feedback from everyone in the group, I said yes. It was
really emotional because I am coming to know Christ
and it is very overwhelming. I am not used to this
deep level of commitment and love and feeling.

November 23, 2003

Lots of big news. Got baptized by Gail in front of the
church. It was a wonderful, freeing moment. This
was just between me and God. Ben had nothing to do
with it. I popped out of the water feeling absolutely
invigorated. Harper said my face looked red! When
we got home from church, Ben surprised me with the
most gorgeous diamond platinum ring that I have ever

seen. I have never owned anything this beautiful in my entire life.

December 2, 2003

I had a wonderful thing happen this morning. I walked out to my car and Ben had put gas and oil in it for the long drive up for my eighth women's retreat at Harold's. As I got ready to leave he gave me a giant bear hug and, holding my face in his hands, he said a beautiful prayer asking God to watch over me as I travel to Maggie Valley, North Carolina to learn whatever it is I am supposed to learn this weekend from Harold and the other women. So, we are turning a new corner in our marriage that includes nurturing and intimacy. It feels great!

Chapter Thirteen. A New Day

❦

The events of 2003 allowed me to finally see how far I had come in my emotional and spiritual reclamation. I knew I had embraced the principles of recovery when the news of Ben's demoralizing relapse did not send me into a long period of hopelessness, resentment, and rage. We both had learned enough about the healing process to know the right way, if there was one, to disclose horrible news. Ben went to Harold and told him about the relapse and agreed to follow his guidelines of disclosure; this was a positive sign of his growth in recovery. Also, his HIV and other blood tests had been done and were there in black and white for me to see. Plus, I had a support system of people waiting in the wings if I needed them to lean on. All these factors buffered me from Ben's relapse. My journal reflects my sense of growth and confidence.

November 10, 2004

Boy, what a difference. A new day. I am actually doing much better. I credit getting out of my own misery and starting a new group in Celebrate Recovery called SOSA (Spouses of Sex Addicts). I have held three meetings, and we have had a new person attend each night. The first night I met a beautiful young woman with three kids, one was a five-month old baby. Her husband had just a month earlier come out to her about his sex addiction. He was into prostitutes, strip clubs, and porno. It's a terrible place to be, as I know too well. Last week there were five women. I feel better knowing I have a purpose with these women and that my experience can be used for something good.

Time had proven that I had grown, and while I continue to this day to hate Ben's dysfunction, I have learned how to love him as a man and as a husband. At the time of this writing, my youngest daughter, Olivia, is graduating from high school.

A few days before her graduation, Ben and I met Harper and the graduate-to-be at El Cerro, at one of our favorite Mexican restaurants.

There we were with my daughters, Harper and Olivia, speaking almost fluent Spanish to an impressed young waiter. My husband, who was in a goofy mood, said the following sentence with complete sincerity and the same kind of seriousness he would pay to a patient awaiting important test results: *Lavander an del hotel, zapatos con frijoles y un plato de jalapeño iglesisas, por favor.*

Ben, standing six-feet-two and weighing two hundred pounds, with dark skin and dark eyes, exudes an air of authority with a slight touch of arrogance. He is my husband, a man I have hated, a man I have loved. And he had just intentionally ordered, *Laundry of the hotel, shoes with beans, and a plate of jalapeño churches.* Please.

Harper and Olivia knew what was coming when Ben closed his menu and he peered innocently at the waiter. They began giggling, raising their hands to cover their wide grins. Because none of the words made sense, save for maybe *frijole* or *jalapeño*, the waiter was momentarily puzzled. Their laughter gave it away, and Ben finally pointed out an entrée on the menu.

We rarely ate together anymore. Even with Harper attending Coastal Carolina nearby and her apartment less than ten miles away, we hardly saw her. I had been at the house putting a few finishing touches on a new piece of furniture I'd been painting when Olivia called from school.

"We're getting out early," she said. "The last day of school is only a half day. We should all go to lunch."

"Call Harper," I said. "Maybe she can meet us over at El Cerro. I'll call your dad."

Ben's new schedule had him working half-days on Fridays and through the miracle of cell phones, we all pulled up into the parking lot, arriving from different directions, in different cars, to enjoy lunch together. That word *together* is not lost on me. After so many awful weeks and months and years, it felt like nothing short of a miracle.

Family is a precious and fragile thing, and after what my family and I have been through, I will never again take any member for granted. It is a wonderful place to be in—to love my husband and have my family intact, to actually look forward to enjoying sharing a meal together.

And enjoy it we did, laughing so hard with one another. We were discussing graduation plans as the plates were cleared, the four of us planning the rest of the afternoon as the young waiter slid the check in front of Ben. The girls were realizing that their parents were getting older as their father checked his pockets for his reading glasses, finally pushing the bill across the table to me.

"You're blind," I said.

"You have all the money anyway," he responded.

My girls, both having spent summers waitressing in local restaurants, made sure I tipped the waiter generously and signed the correct copy for the restaurant. They were responsible and beautiful, the both of them, even though they still foraged through my bag for gum-ball money as we exited the restaurant. I worried for a moment that they would choke on those massive balls of sugar—these were the extra large gum balls. I was their mother and they were still my little girls, regardless of their ages.

We walked outside to the parking lot, content not only from our food but from being together. For that day, we were still intact and better for it.

My kids had grown up, all four of them. Having Olivia get ready to go to college gave my heart a mixture of fear over being alone with Ben and excitement over having the freedom of an empty house. I have my furniture painting, I have Ben, and I have my recovery life. I can really focus on what I want to do, I said to myself.

Ben and I were gearing up to do another presentation of our testimonies later that night at a local church. We have grown familiar with this routine, but each time we speak, our individual stories have changed a bit, reflecting growth and setbacks. We have been happy and humbled to share our story with people who are hungry for insights and hope.

Roughly ten years earlier, I had been told that we only had a two percent chance to stay married. There we were, however, three months away from our twenty-fifth wedding anniversary, preparing to tell our story together and show people that, yes, doing the work of recovery is worthwhile. By giving our testimony, by allowing people in pain to see our faces and listen to our words, we prove that no person or couple is just another statistic.

Through the sheer force of wills, both mine and Ben's, plus the multiple, top-notch therapy and spiritual guidance we have had, we saw those silly numbers swayed to our favor.

"Good evening, my name is Ben, I am believer in Jesus Christ, and I am a sex addict," Ben said to the large gathering.

"And my name is Maurita," I said as I stood next to him, sharing the same microphone. "I am a believer in Jesus Christ, and I got into recovery because of the trauma of my husband's sexual addiction."

Then Ben continued: "By God's grace and the healing power of Jesus Christ, I am standing here today. I'd like to tell you my story of how I used lust and sex to escape from feelings of shame, fear, and inadequacy, about a life of self-absorption and self-centeredness that nearly cost me my marriage and everything meaningful to me. I want to tell you how God, through his love and grace, has supernaturally transformed my life and my marriage.

"I was born in a resort town in New Jersey and raised in a Jewish family. From early childhood, I felt that I was not good enough, smart enough, or likeable. I was always afraid that I would embarrass myself or 'choke' when I had to perform. I had an overwhelming feeling of shame and fear of failure. From as early as I can remember I felt uncomfortable with my feelings and emotions. Somehow I learned that expressing sadness, hurt, or loneliness was embarrassing, I felt that people would make fun of me for showing emotion.

"I was a kid with a lot of character. Outwardly, I was funny and talkative; inwardly, I had to perform for everyone to feel accepted. For me the only safe place was fantasy. I could isolate into a world of fantasy where I could be anyone or do anything without the fear of failure and humiliation. As a young boy I was a constant underachiever, that way no would expect too much of me. I was unwilling to try too hard at anything because my fear of failure was so overwhelming and humiliating. I felt most comfortable and in control when I was breaking rules, undermining authority, or causing some kind of trouble.

"I wanted to be known as the kid that would accept any dare, take any risk, or do anything that most people were afraid to do. This made me feel special. I had no fear of failing in these areas of my life since I had a knack of talking my way out of consequences.

"At the age of nine I was exposed to graphic pornographic photographs by an adult who was a family friend. I still remember every one of those pictures and how they made me feel. I remember the excitement and curiosity of what those people were doing with their bodies, and I remember the exhilaration of masturbating to those images that have been forever etched in my mind.

"This was the beginning of a lifetime of preoccupation with pornography and masturbation. This became my escape from reality. No matter how bad I felt about myself, or angry and upset I was, I could always find relief by escaping into pornography, sexual fantasy, and masturbation.

"My adolescent and high school years were productive in academics and sports. I also discovered alcohol and drugs. I sought approval from my peers by seeking high-risk behaviors and sexual promiscuity. Anger mixed with depression gave me the courage to do things I ordinarily wouldn't do. I was incapable of having meaningful relationships and was terrified of intimacy or expressing my feelings. I could only relate to the opposite sex physically. My only interest was to act out those graphic images that were locked in my brain.

"After graduating, I went on to college and eventually medical school. I was socially immature and continued to seek approval from all the wrong people for all the wrong reasons. I pursued sexual relationships as a way to compensate for my fear of intimacy. During periods of increased stress during my medical training my sexual acting out increased in frequency and variety. I knew I had a problem but I was too afraid to ask anyone for help. Maybe a steady girlfriend would settle me down.

"I started dating the woman who would eventually become my wife, but I continued to have sexual encounters from the very beginning of our relationship. I finished medical school and went right into residency training. After a few years I got married and eventually opened a medical practice in Myrtle Beach. I wanted to be successful, have a good reputation, make lots of money, and have a family. God gave me everything that I asked for: a wonderful wife who loved me, four beautiful children, professional success, and wealth.

"All of these blessings were not enough for me. I continued using drugs and sex to escape from responsibility. Even with all the success, I still felt that nagging fear and shame about who I really was: doing the right thing didn't feel right. Sexual adventures seemed to be more gratifying even though I was putting everything important to me at risk. The excitement of secrecy and rolling the dice hoping to avoid HIV or other sexually transmitted diseases became more important to me than my family.

"My success story did eventually come to an end. As I enjoyed more professional and financial success, my sexual appetite also increased. I had cultivated the appearance of a professional and family man while at the same time I had a whole other secret life of sexual behavior that was unknown to my wife, family, and close friends. Eventually, I began losing control of my two lives. My sexual encounters were no longer satisfying, and I had to increase my frequency and engage in riskier behaviors in order to get my fix.

"My business and finances were starting to fail and my marriage was beginning to unravel. Suicide became an option. I didn't care much about myself, but I did love my wife and children. I wanted help but I was afraid to ask. I just didn't see any hope for me.

"My wife was at the end of her rope. She had enough of my coming home in the middle of the night reeking of cigarettes and alcohol and hearing my lies about seeing patients at the hospital. Her suspicions and my denials were driving her into rage. Finally, she said, get help or get out.

"I sought help from a counselor who convinced me that I had a sexual addiction. I was admitted to a treatment center and I told my wife that I had a drug and alcohol problem. The hardest day of my life came on the day that I disclosed to her about my sex addiction and twenty years of infidelity," Ben said, as he finished. He cleared his throat and stepped back.

I stepped toward the microphone and began speaking. "My husband called me a few days after entering rehab and asked me to read a book called *Out of the Shadows* by Patrick Carnes," I told them. My testimony didn't go all the way back to childhood, like Ben's did. I started during the time Ben made his disclosure to me.

"It was a book about sexual addition," I continued. "I had never heard of such a thing and couldn't imagine why he would want me to read about something so dark and sick. The only thing I identified with was that maybe he had a problem with masturbation, as he and his friends sometimes joked openly about it.

"Then, about a week into his treatment program he called me and told me he now understood what was wrong with him. He said he was an alcoholic, drug addict, and a full-blown sex addict. That he had been a sex addict since the day we met and it had flourished during our fourteen-year marriage. He then said I needed to get tested for HIV."

"I dropped the phone and fell to my knees. For a few moments, I had the sensation of falling down a black hole with nothing to support or help me. I believe now that I was falling into Hell on Earth. I went into shock and after a few minutes hung up the phone. I realized that night that the one person who I should have been able to count on to guard my heart, my very life, did not exist and never had during my entire married life.

"I went to see Ben a few days later and met with his treatment team. I had decided that if he had not raped anyone or touched a child, I would not start divorcing him until he made it through a suggested three months of in-patient treatment. At this time, one of his doctors gave me more grim news. Ninety-eight percent of marriages fail at this level of addiction and, because of the scope and length of time of my husband's addiction, he had a 95 percent chance of a sexual relapse within five years.

"I returned to Myrtle Beach a truly broken woman. My little family immediately became the subject of mean-spirited gossip and conjecture, some of it at the hands of our friends. Some of my husband's medical colleagues and business treated me with disrespect and cruelty during his absence.

"I believe that sexual addiction is a disease of the soul. It destroys the integrity and self-respect of the men who are acting out, and it destroys the spirit and rips a gaping hole right through the heart of the women who love them. It runs the gamut from Internet pornography, strip clubs, voyeurism, and prostitution to the extremes of rape and pedophilia. I will say to you at this time that my husband looked me in the eyes and lied to me hundreds of times. He betrayed me to the depth of my soul.

"Having to be a responsible mother to four young children probably saved my life and my sanity. I immediately started seeing a loving and aggressive therapist twice a week. His first assignment for me was to go to Al-Anon. It is through Al-Anon that I started my spiritual recovery. It became a safe place for me to share my agony, my shame, and my fear. I cried every day that first year. I had so much grief—grief for the death of my marriage and the dreams for my family. Most of all I grieved for my broken heart and shattered spirit, both as a woman and a wife."

Ben moved back to the microphone. "The three months I spent in a treatment center were the most important time of my recovery," he told the crowd. "The sexual addiction was broken, and I began looking inwardly for the first time in a safe and nurturing environment. I learned about a loving and merciful Higher Power and began seeking a relationship with Him. The hard part was returning home to my wife, Maurita. Her pain and hurt from my betrayal was almost unbearable to watch, and her resentment toward me was huge. I did not see how our marriage could possibly withstand this amount of damage.

"I turned to my Higher Power, went to recovery meetings, and prayed for the strength to endure and remain committed to recovery and to my marriage. Then, some strange things started to happen. Suddenly Christian men, some good friends whom I'd known for years and some just acquaintances, started calling me relentlessly, out of the blue, meeting with me, taking me out to lunch, and sharing with me their faith and telling me about Jesus Christ.

"At first I was intrigued, growing up as a Jew and having my own belief system about Christianity and Jesus, but as time went by, I started reading the Bible and came to believe that Jesus came to this earth to save me. I was baptized and started getting involved in several Bible studies and accountability groups. I started a new relationship with my true Higher Power, Jesus Christ.

"Our marriage began to improve. I was doing well in recovery, leading Twelve Step groups and experiencing some wonderful gifts of peace, serenity, and joy in my marriage, my family, and career. Our church started Celebrate Recovery and I was asked to be a part of leadership and organization. I believe God found a place for me in the church where my addiction could be used for something good. Life was really turning around for me and I was enjoying my connection with a church home and feeling a sense of purpose," Ben said. Once again, he stepped away from the podium, and I moved back to the microphone.

"The next five years revolved around the recovery of my heart and my spirit and, eventually, my marriage," I said, looking out at the audience. It was a nice-sized crowd, and I could see some familiar faces looking back at me. "I sought help through our church, meeting and hanging out with Christian women. I regularly attended Al-Anon, S-Anon, and private therapy sessions. I even entered a five-week, in-patient treatment center where they specialized in trauma and sex addiction.

"Our marriage made it beyond the five-year mark without a relapse so I believed we'd beaten the odds. This belief was short-lived. In April of 2003 I was asked to meet with my husband and his therapist. What happened next is in recovery circles known as a disclosure. My husband gave me a detailed, agonizing account of a relapse that had occurred months earlier on a trip out of town. Once again, I sat and listened to some things that no wife should ever, ever have to hear from her husband. To say I was shocked and devastated is an understatement.

"Our therapist has said many times over the years that addiction can be cunning, baffling, and powerful. He added a new word that day. He added the word *patient*. 'Maurita,' he said. 'Your husband's addiction was patient.'

"I called our senior pastor and met with him in his office. Heartbroken and full of despair, I told him the marriage was over and that the relapse was a sign from God to run for my life. Ronnie said he believed that God would not bring our marriage along so far only to have it destroyed by this one incident. So I asked him, 'What is God trying to teach me?'

"Ronnie looked at me with such kindness and conviction in his faith and said, 'Maurita, I would love to tell you what I think God is trying to teach you but that is not for me to say. The great challenge for you is to find out that answer on your own.'

"Well, that was not what I wanted to hear. I wanted his blessing for a divorce. Instead, Ronnie and his wife, Gail, challenged me to face my pain and hopelessness head on, and to keep an open mind and heart to what God wanted me to learn.

"I went back into therapy and into more painful soul-searching. It wasn't long before two important truths emerged. First, God's message to me concerning the relapse was this: *I don't want you to divorce at this time, I want you to come closer to Me, my precious daughter.* Second, I came to the realization that both my husband and myself brought a lot of dysfunction and emotional baggage into this marriage. I had a serious inability to be emotionally intimate, just like my husband. Our methods for coping with the emptiness and fear just manifested themselves differently in our adult lives.

"I stood on a stage much like this one a couple of years ago and said that I would divorce my husband if he ever relapsed. At the time, I meant it. I simply never thought I could ever survive the emotional trauma of living through a relapse. But a beautiful thing has happened on this road to recovery and that is I have a spiritual foundation that has become a source of strength for me that I didn't have when I started this journey. I have a small, trusted network of men and women I can lean on in times of trouble. Within the last two years I went through the Twelve Steps of Celebrate Recovery with my dream team of Christian women, and I got baptized in front of our church community by my spiritual mentor, Gail.

"My husband's sex addiction has been the catalyst that brought me to my knees, brought me to Christ, and, miraculously brought me to a place where my darkest hours and experiences can be used in a positive way.

"I stand before you today a woman who has been profoundly changed by what has happened in my life and marriage. By God's grace I believe I am becoming a woman of substance and depth of mind and heart. I am certainly more compassionate and I am able to extend a hand to other women who are surely to follow some of the paths I have had to walk.

"I would like to close my portion of our testimony today by challenging some of the women in our audience. My challenge to you is this: Do not live one more day of your beautiful, God-given life carrying the burdens of shame, humiliation, or fear by what is going on behind the closed doors of your marriage or relationship. Thanks to groups like SOSA, Celebrate Recovery, and national organizations like S-Anon and COSA, you have a safe place to come and share the truth about your life. For me, being able to meet with a group of women once or twice a week who understand my life as perhaps few can, and who do not judge me for my feelings and behavior, has been a major part of my healing process," I said, and then stepped away from the microphone.

Ben stepped back to the podium again. "My relapse was another critical point, both in my recovery and in my relationship with God," he told the crowd. "God's patience and love for me is unfailing, even when I mess up. I truly felt his compassion and his spirit nudging me back on track and giving me the courage to confess my sins to Maurita and to ask for her forgiveness. I came to fully recognize how I have put my wife, the one person whom I love and who has dedicated her life and heart to me, through unimaginable pain. What I've done to her by breaking our marriage vows and lying and betraying her is unforgivable by human standards. I know today that it is only through God's grace that Maurita was eventually able to forgive me.

"I have learned not to take my recovery program for granted. I have learned that I am just as vulnerable to a relapse when things are going well as when they're not. I've learned that I cannot dabble in my addiction, thinking I can handle a look here or a peek there at a woman or a magazine. Today, I am so afraid to awaken the beast of lust and temptation that I run whenever possible, whenever I feel that old familiar surge of excitement and anticipation.

"Today, God has set me free from the cages of sex addiction. He has restored my sanity, and he has resuscitated a marriage that was terminal. When I look in to the eyes of this wonderful woman, I know that she is God's greatest gift to me. God used my wife as an instrument to lead me into recovery and to find him. Today, God is using the hurt that Maurita and I have both experienced for something good: To offer hope to other suffering sex addicts and their spouses.

"Maurita and I are very grateful for the opportunity to share our story with you today. The gift God has given Maurita and me is shown through opportunities like today, where we can grow together while we share our experiences with all of you. We are grateful you are here and we pray that the blessings we are receiving from God can be poured over to anyone who hears us today, anyone who is struggling with sex addiction or living with a spouse or family member who is sexually addicted and suffering in painful silence. We pray that today will be a turning point in your life and that God offers you hope and a new freedom. Thank you for listening to our story."

My journal reflected a new sense of purpose. I was finally enjoying the sense of gratitude that so many people with long-term recovery promise to people early in recovery.

February 15, 2005

...It is always a humbling and uplifting experience when, together, we tell our story. In a way, which I haven't quite figured out, it makes me love him more, and it just feels so right that we are still married, standing side by side.

After this particular testimony, we also presented a workshop to address sexual addiction in marriage from both points of view. We each wrote our own information and printed out about twenty copies to give out to people who came into our seminar. We couldn't believe it; the people just kept coming in. We ran out of chairs and handouts. We allowed for a question-and-answer period at the end, and we easily could have done a two-hour seminar, one on basic information and statistics, the other for questions and answers. I liked the question-and-answer part the best. The day was very gratifying and I think we worked well together.

A few days later I wrote this in my journal.

February 17, 2005

…We had a nice morning the other day. Instead of making love, I said I wanted to talk. I told him how frustrated I was because I can identify two passions: I love painting and being creative, but I also enjoy supporting women who are battling codependency and sex addiction in their marriages. So, how can I live a life that is fulfilling while bringing both of these together in a meaningful way? I don't have a clue. Ben said I should write a book and that I have a gold mine of material with my journals. So I went to Barnes and Noble and bought some sample books and am now seriously exploring that possibility.

April 10, 2005

…Still at another real turning point in my life. I have no idea what I am supposed to be doing. Is it writing a book about my experiences or what? Go back to school and get a graduate degree, but in what? Paint stuff and open my own place? I still have so much work to do on myself.

...Ben and I are doing well. We are off to Dallas Thursday through Sunday for Ben's first medical conference for addiction medicine. I am going because we are getting along well and I am enjoying him again, and I want to start meeting people who are on the frontlines of addiction.

April 16, 2005

...Another day in Dallas. We have had a really nice trip. I am enjoying being with Ben. We have had some good conversations. We talked about me writing a book again as well as plans for the house and landscaping versus moving out and buying a new house. I am looking forward to going home. I have a lot to look forward to....

As I finish the final revisions for this book, I can't help but recognize what has happened during the process of writing my manuscript. Many high-profile cases of marital betrayal and sexual dysfunction have been made public.

I wish I could tell other women in similar circumstances that there will be a day when everything stops being painful, that Ben is a perfect spouse, and that my fears have all been washed away. I wish I could tell you that we live in a forgetful or kinder society that allows privacy during painful times. But we don't. I wish I could tell you that my marriage is finally perfect, that it is unbreakable and it will stand the test of time. It isn't. That is not how recovery works. Each day is new, and each day requires the strength and conviction of the day before.

Early on, I could not understand or even begin to comprehend what people in recovery meant when at meetings they made comments, "I am grateful for the addict in my life." When I heard that, I would sit on metal folding chairs and silently roll by eyes while thinking to myself, *These women are crazy! How could I possibly be thankful for marrying a man who broke my heart?* Nevertheless, more than a decade later, I marvel at my life as it now is, and I am finally able to understand what people in recovery mean when they say that.

Through my deepest, most shattering pain has come my greatest growth as a human being. Crushing fear and despair forced me to seek out the truth about my life and my marriage. My husband's sexual addiction brought me to my knees and extinguished my life as I knew it to be. This sometimes agonizingly slow journey has led me out of the depths of darkness and into an exciting emotional and spiritual renewal that is still at work in my life today.

I can now honestly say, *I am happily married to the same man I married twenty-seven years ago.* That is, quite simply, a miracle.

I will never be the same woman I was before this happened. This is a good thing, because I would not want to be her again. Certainly, I will always look back on those years with a sense of sadness and loss. But it was also a time of self-discovery and reawakening. It has become a part of me, and I am making peace with that. I tend to look at this great challenge I faced with a new sense of satisfaction. I have done battle with the destruction and grief that sexual addiction has caused me, and I am winning the war.

Chapter Fourteen. Eight Challenges to Consider

୫୬

Over the years, I have noticed that most women share some common questions and concerns related to sex addiction. This chapter discusses what I call the Eight Challenges.

They are

- Do you need to know the details?
- The wedding ring
- How do you forgive your husband for one of life's ultimate betrayals?
- Holidays, anniversaries, and birthdays
- How a father impacts a woman's life
- The impact on our children
- How do I trust my husband again?
- Finding a spiritual mentor

I have found that writing my thoughts and feelings on paper has been an integral part of my personal healing and growth. I encourage you to find a quiet, comfortable place and do some writing in a separate notebook or journal. No one has to read your writing except you. All you have to do is this: Be willing, be honest, be open.

Challenge One: Do You Need to Know the Details?

This question comes up a lot, especially during the beginning of the recovery journey. Every woman is different. Some of us want to know everything and some of us don't have a need to know anything more.

For me, I wanted to know really specific details. Sometimes my imagination was worse than what my husband actually did, so, in those few cases, it was a positive thing for me to ask. At other times, his answers were worse than I imagined. I do remember that almost every time I asked a question and my husband answered honestly, it was as if a knife took a little cut out of my heart, a little chip out of my soul.

A simple question like, "What did you do with your wedding ring when you were out looking for sex?" turned into something so much more painful. His response was, "I put it in my pocket." Then I would imagine him making a conscious decision to take it off, so that meant he knew what he was doing. (He wasn't too drunk or too stoned because he was sober enough to decide.) I would think about him putting his wedding ring back on. Did he do that in the driveway or walking up the front steps to our house? What was going on in his brain as he put the ring back on? Did he ever think of me or the kids? How could he possibly walk into our bedroom, take off his clothes, and get into bed with me right after sexually acting out? Thoughts like these were agonizing. Sometimes, asking them only opened the door for more pain.

No one knows what is right for you to ask but you. I would encourage you to follow your heart on this one. Please remember, if you are prepared to ask the question—then you have to be prepared to hear and absorb the answer.

Questions to consider:
1. Before asking anything specific, have you run your questions by someone you trust, such as a sponsor, therapist, or spiritual mentor?
2. Are you prepared to really hear the answer to your questions?
3. What are your deal breakers, your bottom line behaviors that you just can't accept?
4. Have you thought through what you will do if you hear something that is a deal breaker for yourself?

I encourage you to get emotional support in place before you ask the tough stuff. Call a trusted friend and let him or her know what you are preparing to do. Let that person know you may need to call on him or her after the fact. Knowing I now have that safety net makes a world of difference. I am not afraid to confront and I am not afraid that I will have no one to count on in the event of a crisis.

If you are a woman who is dealing with your husband's serious sexual addiction, I encourage you to take special care with this issue. Some things we might hear are truly dark and traumatic. I know this subject well because a large part of my post-traumatic stress disorder was directly related to how I found out and what I found out about my husband's behavior. It is so difficult for those of us who aren't in that lifestyle to begin to comprehend what goes on with sex addiction.

For this subject, I wish you courage and, ultimately, peace.

Challenge Two: The Wedding Ring

I took my wedding ring off the night I found out about my husband's sexual betrayal and I never put it back on. My wedding ring was supposed to represent a special, unbreakable bond between Ben and me. The moment I felt the horror of my husband's infidelity, I didn't feel married anymore. That ring symbolized a fraud. It was given to me under fraudulent circumstances.

A year or two into recovery, my therapist told me that not wearing a ring on my left hand was damaging to my marriage. It took a long time for me to begin wearing a ring again, because it was a private and public statement that says, "I am a married woman." I had to feel married, not just look married. I never did put on my original ring again. We bought a new, simple gold band instead. My original ring will not be handed down to our children, even after all this time. In my eyes, it represents something evil. I still have not decided exactly what to do with the ring.

Questions to consider:
1. How do you feel when you look at your wedding ring?
2. What do you think of when you think about the day of your wedding?

To wear or not to wear a ring was a difficult part of my emotional recovery. My intent was not to punish or embarrass Ben. My heart didn't heal as fast as other people would have liked. If this is a struggle for you, follow your heart and take the time to heal.

Challenge Three: How Do You Forgive Your Husband for One of Life's Ultimate Betrayals?

I forgave my husband through agonizingly ruthless, hard work and time. I needed time to lick my wounds, time to grieve, time to really look at myself, and time to get honest with myself. I needed time to think about what I really wanted, deserved, and expected out of a husband. I should have done these things before I agreed to marry Ben.

Being able to truly forgive Ben took more than three years. I had to go through the stages of shock, grief, rage, resentment, unwillingness, and fear to even have the desire to want to forgive him. First, I had to reach a stage of eventual acceptance and a willingness to put his betrayal in the past and stop throwing his old behaviors in his face when we argued about current issues.

Our therapist, Harold, and some of our closest friends who were privy to what was going on would tell me, "Maurita, you have to forgive him or divorce him and move on." My standard retort would be, "Well, give me a lobotomy. Then I can forgive him."

I remained in what I call the "Desert of Forgiveness" for a long time. Intellectually, the notion of forgiveness came easier. My true heart-healing took much longer.

Forgiving Ben took a couple of different routes. First, through Gail, I came to realize that God had already forgiven Ben. Ben had literally gotten on his knees and asked for forgiveness—in the company of other Christian men. He prayed for forgiveness—for his betrayal and what he had done to me and his family. In God's eyes, Ben had been forgiven, but I still clung to a state of unforgiveness. I was holding on to something even Ben was released from. How crazy is that?

I wish I could share with you that I had a lightning-bolt moment when I actually forgave Ben and I found peace. It did not come that way for me; it only came with time.

I needed time to decide that I wanted to forgive him, and I needed time to decide when it was in my best interest—not his—to forgive Ben. I needed time to learn and accept that sexual addiction was actually a disease.

In addition, time spent with my spiritual mentor, Gail, was critical for understanding forgiveness from a Biblical standpoint. Gail and I had many discussions about this subject. The great thing I remember about this piece in this process was she never said, "You have to forgive." Instead, she gave me clear Biblical examples of how Christ handled betrayal and specific scripture references of what we are to do, as humans, when we are confronted with the challenge of forgiving the unforgiveable.

To be able to say, "I forgive you," and actually feel and mean it from your heart is tough. But I am here to tell you it can be done. I know, because I have done it.

Questions to consider:
1. Do you want to forgive your husband?
2. Do you believe he deserves to be forgiven?
3. Are you waiting for something from him, in order for you to forgive him?
4. Do you forgive yourself for marrying him in the first place?
5. Do you forgive yourself for not realizing what was going on behind your back?
6. What does the word *forgiveness* mean to you?

Forgiveness is a huge mountain to climb. Don't ever give up on forgiveness. It will follow you wherever you go on this Earth. One of my favorite Harold sayings is this: "Wherever you go, you will take you with you." This means you can divorce, move to a new town, bury your betrayal, or deny that betrayal had an impact on your spirit as a woman. If you don't face your feelings now, I believe they will surface somewhere else in your life.

If you have finished journaling on this challenge, good for you! Take some time off today and do something fun for yourself. You so deserve it.

Challenge Four: Holidays, Anniversaries, and Birthdays

While growing up in a large, Irish Catholic family we always celebrated the major holidays and family birthdays. The first couple of years of recovery were horrible during holidays. I felt such a sense of sadness and emptiness because our husband-wife connection had been shattered. My sense of my children having a healthy father was gone, so what did we have to celebrate? Weddings were the most difficult of events to face. I went through a long period of thinking that marriage was a giant fraud.

Fortunately, as the years went by I found a sense of gradual healing in this area. During our first couple of years in recovery we tried new traditions and places to celebrate days like Thanksgiving and Christmas. For our first Thanksgiving we served food at a senior citizens center, then went to a friend's house for dinner.

I am happy to report that we are back on track with family celebrations and holidays, and we do it with flourish and excitement. I have done the heart-healing, and I really want to make the effort again.

Questions to consider:
1. What dates or anniversaries cause you to feel sad, resentful, or anxious?
2. Why don't you want to celebrate a certain day?

Here's a challenge for you: If you can't live with old traditions of your family this year, what new traditions can you start instead? This is particularly important to look at if you have children at home. Holidays are stressful enough without a broken heart. Give yourself a break and do the best you can.

Challenge Five: How a Father Impacts a Woman's Life

My father's death in 2001 remains one of the saddest life changes I have had to face. He died at a time in my life when I really could have used his humble wisdom, unyielding integrity, and undeniable love.

I felt his absence most when I faced my husband's relapse. I felt utterly alone.

Thanks to my recovery experiences, I was able to realize early on what a critical relationship the father-daughter connection is and the impact my father has had on my life. My impressions of my father and my feelings and life experiences with him have shaped all my relationships with the men I have been close to.

The work I did on myself through recovery changed my relationship, for the better, with my dad. I was able to be open and honest with him in a freeing and loving way.

Helping him through what turned out to be a short, cruel illness and death was an incredibly sad and scary time. My newfound recovery and spiritual-based friends were a great source of comfort during this period of time. My true strength came from my new faith and budding relationship with Christ. Having the personal knowledge of knowing Christ was on my side, plus on my Dad's (he was a believer), gave me a sense of peace and acceptance of his illness and death.

As horrible as my father's death was, it wasn't anywhere nearly as painful as my husband's disclosure of his sexual betrayal. There is a certain natural, circle-of-life experience when a parent dies first. Being betrayed and lied to by your spouse, however, is an unnatural act of life. I believe that is why any form of sexual betrayal is so devastating to the human spirit.

During my father's short illness, he was admitted to the hospital for two or three days. After he had settled into his room, I started feeling inadequate in making him comfortable. I wanted to get his mind off of the seriousness of the day. I asked him if he wanted me to rent some movies or audio books from the hospital gift shop. He said, "No thanks."

"Dad," I said, "I feel badly because I don't want you to be bored or lonely while you are here. What can I do to make you more comfortable?" My father replied, "Well, I am doing exactly what I want to be doing."

Puzzled, I asked, "What is that?"

Without skipping a beat, he answered, "I am spending time with my precious daughter." I was stunned. This was coming from a father who could never hold my face in his hands and tell me he loved me.

My heart pounded and I wanted to jump out of my chair and sing out loud with joy! Yes, he really does love me! I had waited my entire life for my father to look me in the eye and say, "I love you." He died never being able to do that. That moment in his hospital room was a great gift—I finally understood how much he loved me. Just because he couldn't say it did not mean he didn't feel it. It's a moment in time I will cherish forever.

Questions to consider:
1. What is your relationship like with your father?
2. Are you able to identify traits of your father with traits of your husband or boyfriend?
3. How are they alike?
4. How are they different?
5. How does your husband or boyfriend treat his own mother?
6. Do you like what you see? (refers to question 5)
7. Do you have the kind of relationship you want to have with your father?
8. What are you willing to risk to heal this relationship?

If the relationship you have with your father is an issue for you, I encourage you to dive in and face whatever ails it. My changed relationship with my father brought me peace, growth, and insight. I hope, after you have done this work, it will bring you similar peace, emotional growth, and insight.

Challenge Six: The Impact on Our Children

When I first started therapy, I would assure my therapist that the kids "really didn't hear or know that much," that we pretty much hid what was going on. "Yeah, right," Harold's response would always be. "Your kids know more than you think they know." He was right. My children were twelve, ten, nine, and six when this addiction was revealed to me.

Here is what I now know. My oldest children clearly remember my yelling at Ben when he came home late at night. He always seemed to be in a calm, almost taunting mood. I, on the other hand, would be beside myself with worry and fear about his whereabouts. I would be flooded with relief that he was home safe, but then I would immediately fly into a screaming rage. My children only remember hearing my loud, angry voice. To them, Dad was the nice parent, Mom was the mean one.

Once I found out about Ben's behavior, I changed into a sad, broken-hearted mom who cried all the time. I thought I did it privately, or when they were asleep. The reality is they heard me crying many of those nights, deep in my grief.

They had a mother who all but completely withdrew from most family activities. For a long time I refused to do anything as a family. I wanted nothing to do with their father, and I had no desire to be seen in public as a family. Although I tried to keep my angry, sarcastic barbs at Ben out of earshot of the kids, I know today that they heard those comments.

As our children grew, they gradually learned more about what their father's addiction was. At times, they were angry and disgusted with Ben and his behavior. At other times, they have been sickened and confused by my decision to stay married to him.

I have good news. One of the great things about our recovery process is the work we have done as parents. We have realized that providing a unified front has given our kids a gift of real stability and security in their home—something they didn't really have before recovery. We learned to stand as one parental voice, not allowing our children to play off the weaker parent. When there is a serious discussion or decision that needs to be made, we discuss it privately so the kids don't hear us disagree. Ben and I have made a conscious effort to be more respectful of each other in front of our kids. We try and put our marriage first and our children second. Olivia, our youngest child, paid us a great compliment last year. She said, "Why couldn't you guys have waited until I got out of high school to get into recovery?" We are better parents because of the problem solving we did to save our marriage.

Now I am going to encourage you to think about some very tough stuff.

1. I want to encourage you not to tell your children your problems. There are things about sex addiction that should be shared with children at age-appropriate times. Decide what to tell the kids with a counselor or someone you trust to give you sound spiritual, emotionally-appropriate advice.
2. I want to encourage you to avoid getting your children to pick sides. You could possibly be doing this by playing the victimized wife or by putting your husband down in front of your kids. Instead of bringing them in on your adult problems, take these comments and feelings to a friend or to an S-Anon meeting.

I found this particular challenge very difficult to do. There were times I failed. I encourage you to remember that no matter what your husband has done to you and your marriage, he will always be their father. They may be mad and hurt now, but they will always love him no matter what he has done.

Our children have paid a heavy price for what has happened in our home. I do have a sense of peace in knowing that there is a reason why my children were born into this marriage. Just as God knows why sex addiction is in my life, I have to trust that the same thing holds true for my four extraordinary children.

Questions to onsider:
1. Are you telling your children too much information about your spouse's behavior?
2. Are you making disparaging or disrespectful comments about your spouse in front of your children?
3. Are you using your children as a sounding board for your adult problems and pain?
4. What can you do today, as your child's greatest advocate, to change a defeating or negative behavior that is really aimed at your spouse?

Consider how to appropriately communicate with your children. I sat my kids down when I told them that their Dad was going to stay in rehab for a long time. In our case it was three and a half months. I know they were scared and did not understand what was going on. I brought them all together one night and told them they should pick one best friend, someone they trusted, and tell them what was going on at home. I, as their mother, gave them permission to do that. I think that really lessened their loads a bit. Just like I needed a support system, so did my children. I also made it a point to talk to all their teachers and coaches and explain, in very general, non-specific terms, what was going on. I asked them to let me know if they noticed any change in class performance or behavioral changes. I took a proactive approach in this area. In retrospect, this behavior kept me sane and kept me from drowning in my own misery. Realizing I had four little human beings to take care of forced me to step up to the plate.

Challenge Seven: How Do I Trust my Husband Again?

Ah, the trust question. I am often asked questions about trust problems by women who are new to sex addiction. "How long did it take you to trust him?" "How will I know that he isn't lying to me again?" "Will I ever trust him again?" Reestablishing trust was one of the most challenging and difficult mountains I had to climb.

During my first few years of recovery, I had no trust. As a matter of fact, I trusted no one—male, female, family member, or friend. I figured if my own husband lied to me, then why should I believe in anyone ever again? With regard to Ben, I was skeptical and completely untrusting in him. Even if I personally dropped him off at the door of a meeting and picked him up an hour later at the same door, I still didn't believe a word he said. That kind of thinking was one of the many consequences of his lying. My attitude early on was, *If my husband doesn't like me being suspicious, he can leave.*

Ben had to earn back the trust. He did this by being accountable to me—within a certain time limit—at all times. No compromise, no excuses. If he was more than fifteen minutes late he had to call and tell be where he was, who he was with, and when he would be home. He has been tremendous in this area. He has only blown it maybe five times in the last eleven years.

Here is the great thing about how trust plays out in my life today. With my therapist's help, I have re-evaluated my unrealistic expectations of people in general and my husband in particular.

I trust myself first. I have relearned to listen and trust my initial instincts, my gut, and the butterflies in my stomach. I never forget that I am married to an addict. I believe he could act out sexually at any time. Do I think about that or worry about it? No. Never. Thankfully, I have made peace with the issue of trust. I am choosing, this time around, to be in this marriage with Ben, with my eyes wide open to the truth about who he is. I am making a conscious choice to stay and be fully involved in this marriage.

If Ben were to come to me tomorrow and tell me he sexually acted out, I would be at peace with what I would do with our marriage. I am at peace with God and myself with the steps I would take. Do I dwell on that or worry about this happening? No. I have been freed from the burdens of fear and worry about trusting in Ben.

Questions to onsider:
1. Do you trust yourself?
2. In what areas do you struggle with trusting your spouse? Be as specific as possible.
3. What do you think it will take for you to feel safe enough in your relationship to want to start trusting again?

Good for you for taking a closer look at this very tough subject.

Challenge Eight: A Spiritual Mentor

My first spiritual mentor was my senior pastor's wife, Gail. Reaching out to a woman who lived a Christian lifestyle was a real struggle for me. First, I was embarrassed and humiliated to tell a stranger about what had happened in my life. We didn't know each other, and we did not hang out in the same social circles.

I feared that Gail would judge me as a wife and mother for what I had put up with in my marriage. Because her husband Ronnie was a pastor—and a noncheating husband—how could she possibly understand how I felt? After continual prodding from my therapist, Harold, I finally called her to meet face to face.

I still can remember how scared I was when I walked up to her front door and rang her doorbell. It was so awkward, but knowing Harold was sure it would help, I took the risk. Gail lives a block and a half from the ocean, so we decided to walk along the beachfront sidewalk and talk. Two women took a risk and reached out to each other.

Well, guess what? I was wrong in my judgment of her. From our first hour together, when I revealed what had happened in my marriage, she didn't even bat an eye. I mean that literally, because I remember making a conscious effort to look at her face when I told her certain facts. I felt no ridicule from her; I felt safe and knew I had a new ally in my corner.

My relationship with Gail is one of the most life-changing relationships of my life. She is not a therapist, but she intrinsically knew when to push and when to give me my space. She remains a loving friend to whom I can be accountable. Gail will give me honest, compassionate input on the daily dilemmas in my life. She is a mentor without judging and accepts me for who I am. I can ask her anything.

Here is an example of one of our earlier conversations that, in retrospect, makes me laugh.

One day I said, "I think I swear too much." I had never heard Gail use foul language. On the other hand, I have no problem with swearing. I controlled myself around the kids, but I certainly would swear in front of adults. Gail challenged me not to use swear words. So, I asked her, "Instead of using 'asshole' to describe someone, can I use the word 'dickhead' (my favorite)?" Without skipping a beat, she said, "Technically, that is not swearing, but I am going to encourage you not to use that word because it is disrespectful to the person you are saying it to, and it is disrespectful to yourself for using that kind of language." Gulp! Even when she was annoyed with me it was in a loving way.

Questions to consider:
1. Who is your Gail?
2. Who do you know that is more spiritually developed than you?
3. Who do you know that seems to have certain qualities that you want? For instance, Gail had her priorities straight. She did not put her husband first; she put God first in her life. She honored herself and her husband in a healthy way. I wanted to learn how to do that.

Find Your Gail!

Write down three possibilities of women in your life who you might feel comfortable enough to reach out to. Call these women—one by one. Tell them what has happened. Tell them what you need from them. Ask them to mentor you. Do not stop until you find someone who feels like a healthy fit. Remember, you are worth the effort.

In closing, I want to remind you that recovering from a spouse's sex addiction is not a process that you can do on your own. Every year it seems that more professionals, like therapists and clergy members, learn more about how to help people who are in the situation I found myself in. Twelve Step meetings also continue to grow to help sex addicts and their partners. Find the support you need. In time, you will become the support that someone else will need. I wish you strength and peace in your journey.

About the Author

ॐ

Maurita Corcoran has been in the process of recovering her spirit and reclaiming her voice for more than thirteen years. Because of her experiences, she has a new found passion for encouraging other women to do the same. She was instrumental in establishing the first S-Anon group in the Myrtle Beach area and has co-chaired SOSA at Celebrate Recovery. She has led women through the Twelve Steps of S-Anon, and is the founder of the Women's Life Recovery Network, a monthly group that allows women from across the Grand Strand the opportunity to hear one woman's life story. The concept of the group is something she would one day like to see in every community.

Maurita is the mother of four children and is now happily married to her husband of twenty-six years. They reside in Surfside Beach, South Carolina.

A Tribute

ഔൻ

During the roughly ten years of my life upon which this book is based, I have lost some people who made a distinct imprint on shaping the woman I have become. These people include my father, of course; my friends, Jack, Jenny and Keith; and, most painfully perhaps, Charlie McBride.

Charlie was diagnosed with throat and neck cancer in December 2005 at the age of fifty-two, and he died in October 2006 before he could see his fifty-third birthday. His death was a huge blow to my husband and me.

The first time I met Charlie was in the waiting room of my therapist Harold's office. In walks this good-looking, six-foot-guy, with blondish-brown hair; he was wearing hip sun glasses, a flowered shirt, slacks, and expensive European loafers with no socks. He flopped down on a chair next to me and introduced himself. This was Charlie's first time to see Harold; he was fresh out of his third stint in rehab for drug abuse, and he was nervous and could not sit still. He was a funny, nutty ball of energy.

That day was the beginning of a wonderful, authentic, all-too-short relationship. He was a great friend and accountability partner to my husband, challenging Ben to "get real" and not be afraid to show his true self to the rest of the world.

Most importantly, he was the first person who believed in my story and lovingly challenged me to speak out about what happened in my marriage, to talk about sexual addiction when few others were doing so, and to share the miracles that had transpired in my life. He was one of the few people I went to with my fears and doubts and who cared enough about me to tell me the truth about my behavior. Charlie knew I was in the middle of writing this book, but because his health went downhill so horribly fast, I never went to him with my questions or ideas. He was the kind of friend who would do whatever he could whenever I called on him. Recovery can't be all doom and gloom if people like Charlie are a part of it, I sometimes said to myself.

I spent my fiftieth birthday in a Houston, Texas, hospital room finding out that Charlie's cancer had returned with a vengeance and that there was nothing left medically for him to do. Ben, Charlie's wife of a little more than a year, and another of his loyal friends went downstairs for a quick dinner break. I stayed with Charlie alone for a while. He whispered "Mo, can you believe this is happening?" I shook my head, "No," and we both started to weep. Then he whispered, "I am sorry I ruined your birthday." I said, "You didn't ruin my birthday. You have given me a great gift. I will always remember my fiftieth birthday because I will be able to say, "I spent it with my good friend Charlie McBride." We both broke down for a few moments, and I hugged him until we could each collect ourselves.

How can I best honor such a true friend, the one who unknowingly started me on this path of publicly telling my story?

I can honor our relationship by passing on his name along with his philosophy on life: "Think big, outside the box. If you have a dream, a passion for something, go after it. See it through." I can just hear him now that this book is published. "That's great, Mo, congratulations!" he would say, with his thick Southern drawl. "Now, what are you going to do? How are you going to take your life to the next level?"

I am seeing one of my dreams come true, to finish writing a book and hopefully help other women who are walking this road behind me.

So, here's to you, my good friend, Charlie McBride.

The Twelve Steps of S-Anon

ഗ◌ଓ

1. We admitted we were powerless over sexaholism—that our lives had become unmanageable.
2. Came to believe that a Power greater than ourselves could restore us to sanity.
3. Made a decision to turn our will and our lives over to the care of God *as we understood him*.
4. Made a searching and fearless moral inventory of ourselves.
5. Admitted to God, to ourselves, and to another human being the exact nature of our wrongs.
6. Were entirely ready to have God remove all these defects of character.
7. Humbly asked Him to remove our shortcomings.
8. Made a list of all persons we had harmed, and became willing to make amends to them all.
9. Made direct amends to such people wherever possible, except when to do so would injure them or others.
10. Continued to take personal inventory and when we were wrong promptly admitted it.
11. Sought through prayer and meditation to improve our conscious contact with God *as we understood Him*, praying only for knowledge of His will for us and the power to carry that out.
12. Having had a spiritual awakening as the result of these Steps, we tried to carry this message to others and to practice these principles in all our affairs.

S-Anon International Family Groups
P.O. Box 111242
Nashville, TN 37222-1242
(800) 210-8141 or (615) 833-3152
sanon@sanon.org

(The Twelve Steps reprinted and adapted with permission of Alcoholics Anonymous World Services, Inc. Permission to reprint and adapt the Steps and Traditions does not mean that AA is affiliated with this program. AA is a program of recovery from alcoholism—use of this material in connection with programs which are patterned after AA, but which address other problems, does not imply otherwise.)

Acknowledgments

I have heard it said that it takes a village to raise a child. Well, it took a village to help me recover my voice, heal my heart, and reclaim the woman I was meant to be. In order of their appearance, here is my little village. Thank you to my father, who is now an angel, for showing me what courage and integrity looks like here on earth. To my mother, for passing on her passion to create and spirit of loving life. To my sisters and brother, I love you dearly. To Harold Brown, for saving my life, my husband's life, and my family's life. To Gail and Ronnie Byrd, my first spiritual mentors, for seeing me through to the other side. To Joannie and Greg Anderson, for showing me that healthy, loving marriages do exist. To Suzanne and Beth, for finally coming forward. To Barbara, for giving me hope for what was possible. To Scott and Pamela Pyle, for welcoming us into your lives and your home when a lot of other people would not. To Charlie McBride, Lynn Kripple, and Ralph and Cyndi Shamah, for being a phone call away in those early years. To Stuart, for his guidance. To Bob and Lydia Barrows, for their spiritual guidance and personal friendship. To Eddie Dyer, for believing in me and setting me straight. To Corbin and Donna, for not laughing me out of your office.

To the women and men of the Myrtle Beach Al-Anon group, thank you for giving me the opportunity to open my heart to the concept of spirituality. To the courageous women of S-Anon, thank you for showing me time and time again the remarkable resilience of the human spirit. To the women at Gentle Path—Suzanne O'Connor and Amy Campbell—thank you so much for "getting" my story and going to bat for me. To author Cathy Scott, for sharing your writing and editing talents and for listening and understanding what it is I had to say. And to Rebecca Post, my editor at Gentle Path, for believing in my story and bringing it home.

Gentle Path Press

Gentle Path Press was founded in 1998 by Patrick Carnes, Ph.D., a pioneering researcher, clinician, and author in the field of sexual and multiple addictions. Dr. Carnes' goal was to publish innovative books and other resources for consumers and professionals on topics related to addiction, trauma, and brain chemistry. Gentle Path books provide readers with the best research-based materials to help repair the lives of individuals and families.

Dr. Carnes' cutting-edge research and writing became widely known in 1983 with the publication of his book, *Out of the Shadows: Understanding Sexual Addiction*. It was the first book designed to help addicts deal with their sexual compulsions, and to examine the tangled web of trauma, love, addictive sex, hate, and fear often found in family relationships. His research, work with patients, and writing have continued over the past three decades.

Experts and consumers alike have come to embrace Dr. Carnes' 2001 book, *Facing the Shadow: Starting Sexual and Relationship Recovery*, as his most compelling and important work to date. *Facing the Shadow* introduced readers to Dr. Carnes' revolutionary Thirty Task Model for beginning and sustaining long-term recovery.

More information on Gentle Path books can be found at www.gentlepath.com.

Institute for Trauma and Addiction Professionals

Dr. Carnes also founded the International Institute for Trauma and Addiction Professionals (IITAP), which promotes professional training and knowledge of sexual addiction and related disorders. Sex addiction affects the lives of millions of people worldwide, and practicing therapists are on the frontlines treating this epidemic. IITAP offers three distinguished certifications to addiction-treatment professionals: Certified Sex Addiction Therapist (CSAT), Certified Multiple Addiction Therapist (CMAT), and Associate Sex Addiction Therapist (ASAT).

More information can be found at www.iitap.com.